THINK YOU'RE MISTER KNOW-IT-ALL?

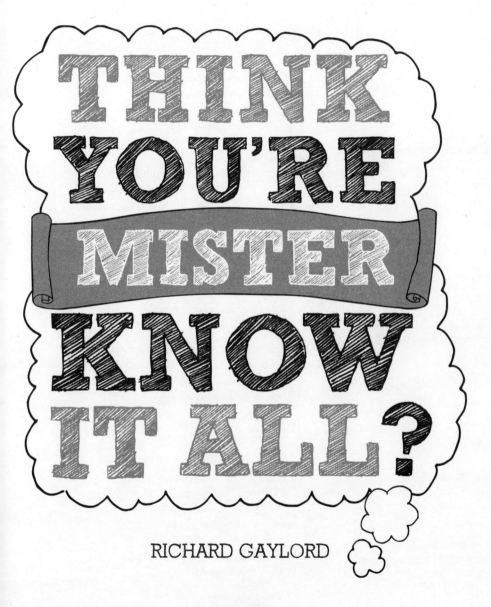

THINK YOU'RE MISTER KNOW IT ALL?

RICHARD GAYLORD

Michael O'Mara Books Limited

First published in Great Britain in 2020 by
Michael O'Mara Books Limited
9 Lion Yard
Tremadoc Road
London SW4 7NQ

A CIP catalogue record for this book is available from the British Library.

Papers used by Michael O'Mara Books Limited are natural, recyclable products made from wood grown in sustainable forests. The manufacturing processes conform to the environmental regulations of the country of origin.

ISBN: 978-1-78929-218-3

1 2 3 4 5 6 7 8 9 10

www.mombooks.com

Designed and typeset by Allan Sommerville

Printed in the UK by CPI Group (UK) Ltd,
Croydon, CR0 4YY

CONTENTS

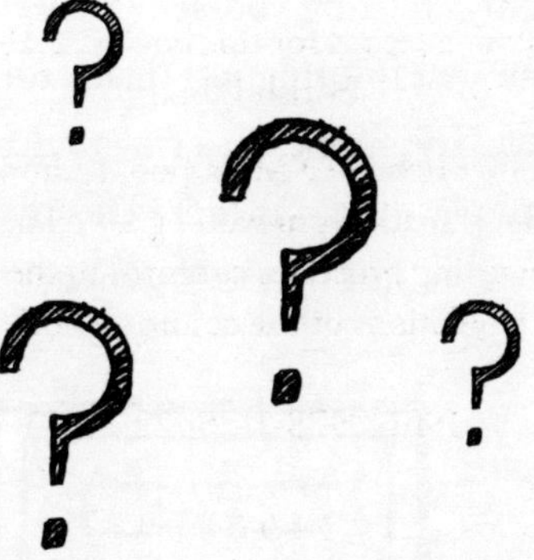

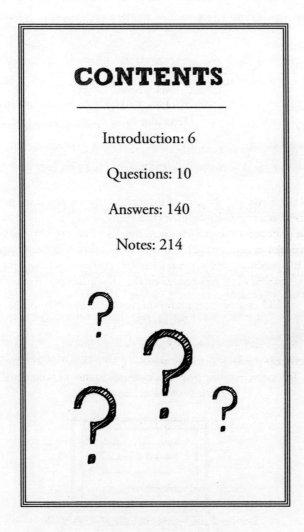

INTRODUCTION

You must have seen them. Those local quiz-night contestants surreptitiously checking their phones under the table before smugly producing the answers. Well, that's no way to win a quiz!

The proper way is, of course, to be such a know-it-all that you can find the correct answer time after time without feeling the need for digital back up. So, is that you? Are you really Mr or Ms Know-It-All? Or are you just looking for a bit of extra fun, and a source of fascinating facts that can win you a quiz, make you look knowledgeable in casual conversations, or impress your friends and family? *

Either way, this is the activity book for you.

Of course, resorting to the internet can also be a way of testing and expanding your knowledge. But as the quizmaster might say, bear in mind that you're only cheating yourself if you do it that way. It's been scientifically proven that information that is too easily accessed is also too easily forgotten. Trying the hard way to dredge up the memories of names, dates and places is a far more effective way of learning than surfing the internet.

* Although, bear in mind that if you're thinking of trying to impress your next date by telling them the names of the seven dwarves or the size of the largest moon of Jupiter, you might want to think again.

This book is a lovingly curated set of quizzes and questions that will test you on how much you really, truly know. From high to low culture, history to geography, science to trivia, television to sports, there's a bit of something from every field all over the world in here.

To be a true know-it-all you need more than just the ability to recall a narrow range of trivia. Some of the quizzes here will test how **complete** your knowledge is: for instance, whether you can name every country in Africa, or the biggest rivers, mountains or animals in the world.

Meanwhile, other sections will probe how **deep** your knowledge is: for instance, if you think you know the Disney movies inside out, then being challenged to name some of the minor characters may make you realize otherwise. And if the flags of the world are your speciality, how about naming every flag that is red, white and blue?

Finally, we will be testing how **broad** your knowledge is, with regular sections of 'twenty questions' on every subject under the sun. And for extra entertainment, the answer sections include fun facts that even the most knowledgeable reader might not know.

The end result should be many hours of fun, as you discover how much you truly deserve the ultimate accolade of being called Mr or Ms Know-It-All.

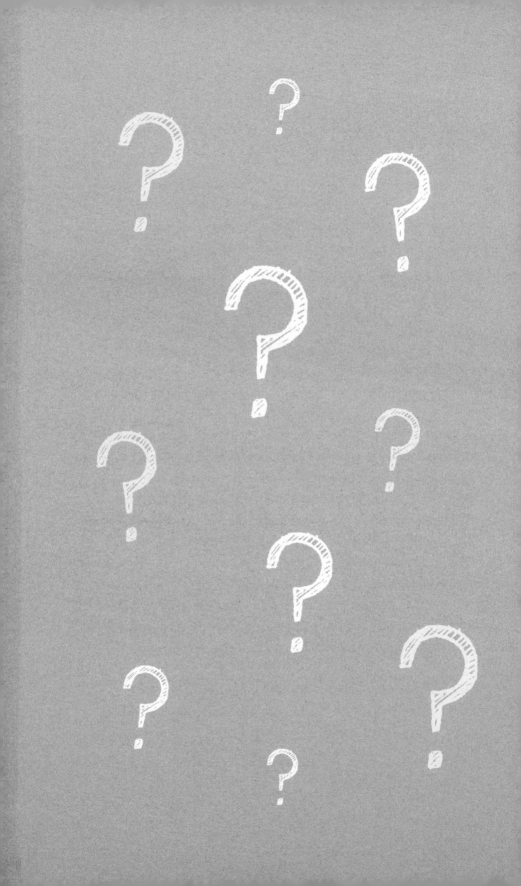

THINK YOU'RE MISTER KNOW-IT-ALL?

The Solar System and its Moons

You probably know the planets of the solar system, but can you list them in order of their size? Bear in mind that Pluto has now been reclassified as a dwarf planet, so it isn't included in this list.

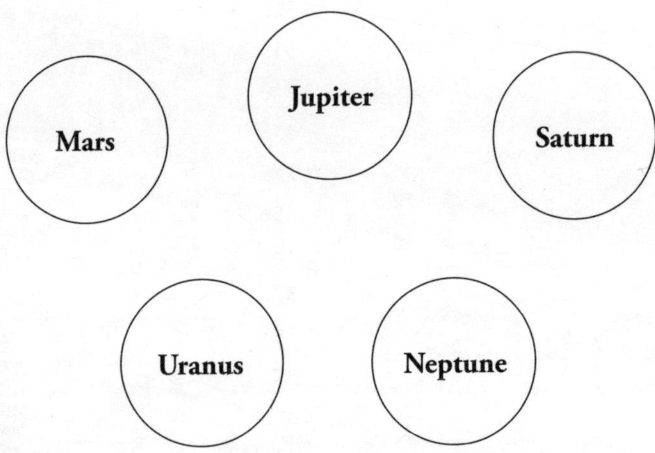

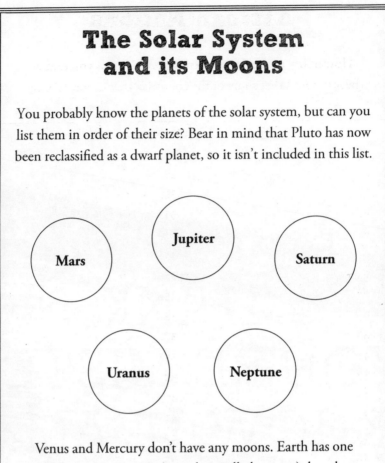

Venus and Mercury don't have any moons. Earth has one (which we are arrogant enough to call *the* moon), but there are plenty more moons in the solar system… Mars has 2, Jupiter has 79, Saturn has 62, Uranus has 27, Neptune has 14 and Pluto (the dwarf) has 5.

Can you name the biggest moon of each?

Answers on page 140

African Nations

How many of the 54 countries of Africa can you name?
(Bear in mind that some of the countries are offshore islands).

1.	**28.**
2.	**29.**
3.	**30.**
4.	**31.**
5.	**32.**
6.	**33.**
7.	**34.**
8.	**35.**
9.	**36.**
10.	**37.**
11.	**38.**
12.	**39.**
13.	**40.**
14.	**41.**
15.	**42.**
16.	**43.**
17.	**44.**
18.	**45.**
19.	**46.**
20.	**47.**
21.	**48.**
22.	**49.**
23.	**50.**
24.	**51.**
25.	**52.**
26.	**53.**
27.	**54.**

Answers on page 140

The Four Elements

Can you name the three members of each group?

Can you name the twelve signs of the zodiac, in their correct order, starting from Aries? The zodiac signs are traditionally grouped into four elements.

1.	**7.**
2.	**8.**
3.	**9.**
4.	**10.**
5.	**11.**
6.	**12.**

Fire Signs	**Earth Signs**
Air Signs	**Water Signs**

Answers on pages 141

Chinese Years

Can you name the twelve animals that make up the Chinese system of labelling years?

In addition, can you say which belongs to each of the four elements of water, earth, wood and metal?

1.

2.

3.

4.

5.

6.

7.

8.

9.

10.

11.

12.

Answers on pages 141

Turning Points in World History

Can you name the dates of the following key moments in global history? There is a hint built in from the start as the events are listed in chronological order. Name the correct year unless the question indicates otherwise.

1. **Unification of China under Emperor Qin Shi Huang, and start of the construction of the Great Wall (*name the correct century*)**
2. **Paul's First Letter to the Thessalonians becomes the earliest known Christian text**
3. **Birth of Muhammad**
4. **Charlemagne, Carolingian King of the Franks and the Lombards, crowned by Pope Leo III as the First Holy Roman Emperor**
5. **Norman Conquest of England**
6. **The First Crusade (*name the correct decade*)**
7. **King Suryavarman II of the Khmer Empire has Angkor Wat built (*name the correct century*)**
8. **The signing of the Magna Carta**
9. **Death of Genghis Khan**
10. **The Ottoman Turks invade Constantinople, defeating the Eastern Roman (Byzantine) Empire**
11. **The printing of the Gutenberg Bible, the first mass-produced book**
12. **First journey of Christopher Columbus to America**
13. **Leonardo da Vinci paints the *Mona Lisa* (*correct decade*)**

14. Conquistador Hernán Cortés starts conquest of the Aztec Empire

15. Ferdinand Magellan's expedition circumnavigates the globe

16. Nicolaus Copernicus's *On the Revolutions of the Celestial Spheres* reintroduces the heliocentric model of the universe (which had earlier been proposed by various ancient Greek thinkers)

17. English colonists establish the first permanent Western settlement in America at Jamestown

18. Start of the English Civil War

19. Publication of Isaac Newton's *Principia Mathematica*

20. The Boston Tea Party

21. The American Declaration of Independence

22. The United Kingdom abolishes the slave trade

23. Napoleon invades Moscow, but is forced to retreat after huge losses

24. Publication of *The Communist Manifesto*

25. Publication of Darwin's *On the Origin of Species*

Answers on page 142

26. Start of the American Civil War

27. The end of Shogun rule in Japan

28. Opening of the Suez Canal

29. Alexander Graham Bell patents the telephone

30. First flight in an aircraft heavier than air, by Orville & Wilbur Wright

31. Einstein publishes the Special Theory Of Relativity

32. The Grand Duchy of Finland is the first country to grant women the right to vote and to stand for political office

33. The Treaty of Versailles is signed

34. End of the Russian Revolution and creation of the Union of Soviet Socialist Republics

35. Wall Street Crash

36. Election of Adolf Hitler as Chancellor of Germany

37. D-Day marks the turning point of World War Two

38. India's independence from the UK

39. Creation of the People's Republic of China under Mao Tse-tung

40. Martin Luther King, Jr. delivers his 'I Have a Dream' speech

41. US President John F. Kennedy is assassinated

42. First message sent on the internet (then known as the ARPANET)

43. Demolition of the Berlin Wall

44. Nelson Mandela elected president of South Africa

45. Al-Qaeda's terrorist attack on the World Trade Towers

Twenty Cartoon Characters

Can you name the date when these classic cartoon characters first appeared?

Mickey Mouse

Donald Duck

Yogi Bear

The Flintstones

Popeye (in print)

Felix the Cat

Betty Boop

Scooby-Doo

Roger Rabbit

The Simpsons (as a separate show)

Beavis and Butthead

The cast of South Park

Hong Kong Phooey

Tom and Jerry

Shrek

Ren and Stimpy

Wile E. Coyote and Road Runner

Foghorn Leghorn

Daffy Duck

Pluto

Answers on page 142

The Movie Appearances of Marilyn Monroe

How many of the movies in which Marilyn Monroe appeared can you name?

At the time of her tragic death Marilyn was working on a movie project which remained unfinished. **Can you name it?**

1.
2.
3.
4.
5.
6.
7.
8.
9.
10.
11.
12.
13.
14.
15.
16.
17.
18.
19.
20.
21.
22.
23.
24.
25.
26.
27.
28.
29.
30.

Answers on page 143

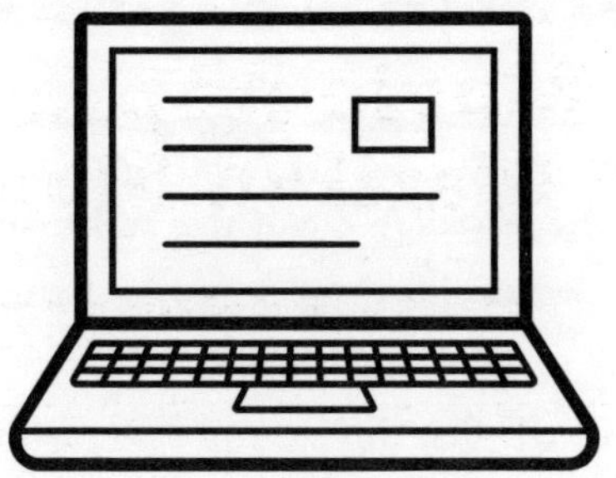

Computer Keyboard

Most of us use a computer every day, but how well are you concentrating?

Can you name the letters of the alphabet from left to right, row by row on a computer keyboard?

Answers on page 144

Fun with Alphabets

How many of the letters A-Z can you write out the Morse code symbol for? (as dots and dashes)

Here are the first three numbers in Morse Code.
1: [dot, dash, dash, dash, dash]
2: [dot, dot, dash, dash, dash]
3: [dot, dot, dot, dash, dash]

Can you deduce (or do you know) the codes for these numbers:

4 5 6 7 8 9 0

How many letters are there in:

The Russian Alphabet

The Greek Alphabet

The Spanish Alphabet

The Japanese Alphabet (using the hiragana or katakana syllabaries rather than Kanji)

The Turkish Alphabet

Answers on page 144

Disney Animals

You may well be able to put all the Disney animated features in the correct order (feel free to try if you want to show off…), but how good are you on the character names?

Can you name the animals in each of the following Disney features?

The owl in *The Sword in the Stone*

The horse and the cat in *One Hundred and One Dalmatians*

The alligator in *Lady And The Tramp*

The tiger in *The Jungle Book*

The mouse in *The Aristocats*

The albatross in *The Rescuers*

The Fox and The Hound

The Lion King's father, mother and uncle

The dragon in *Mulan*

Tarzan's childhood friends, a gorilla and an elephant

Nemo's father in *Finding Nemo*

The sheriff's horse in *Home on the Range*

The loving couple in *The Princess and the Frog*

The reindeer in *Frozen*

Answers on page 144

Quickies

See how fast you can name all of the following:

1. The World's Tallest Building
2. The World's Tallest Mountain
3. The World's Tallest Volcano
4. The World's Longest River System
5. The Deepest Trench in the Oceans
6. The World's Longest Railway
7. The World's Busiest Airport
8. The World's Deepest Lake
9. The World's Longest Road
10. The Three Largest Deserts in the World
11. The Oldest Mountain Range on the Planet

Answers on page 145

Great First Lines

Can you identify which movie these fantastic opening lines of dialogue come from? And can you name the character and the actor that played them?

'As far back as I can remember, I always wanted to be a gangster.'

'We were somewhere around Barstow on the edge of the desert when the drugs began to take hold.'

'Let me tell you what "Like a Virgin" is about...'

'Last night, I dreamt I went to Manderley again.'

'Only ever met one man I wouldn't wanna fight.'

'I had the craziest dream last night. I was dancing the White Swan.'

'Three billion human lives ended on August 29th, 1997. The survivors of the nuclear fire called the war Judgment Day.'

*'Choose Life. Choose a job. Choose a career. Choose a family. Choose a f***ing big television.'*

'The world is changed. I feel it in the water. I feel it in the earth. I smell it in the air.'

'I'm 36 years old, I love my family, I love baseball, and I'm about to become a farmer. But until I heard the voice, I'd never done a crazy thing in my whole life.'

'I remember those cheers. They still ring in my ears.'

'The key to faking out the parents is the clammy hands. It's a good non-specific symptom; I'm a big believer in it.'

'And it's a story that might bore you, but you don't have to listen, because I always knew it was going to be like that.'

'Who am I? You sure you want to know?'

Answers on pages 145

Cultural Symbols

Can you name these auspicious or significant symbols from cultures around the world?

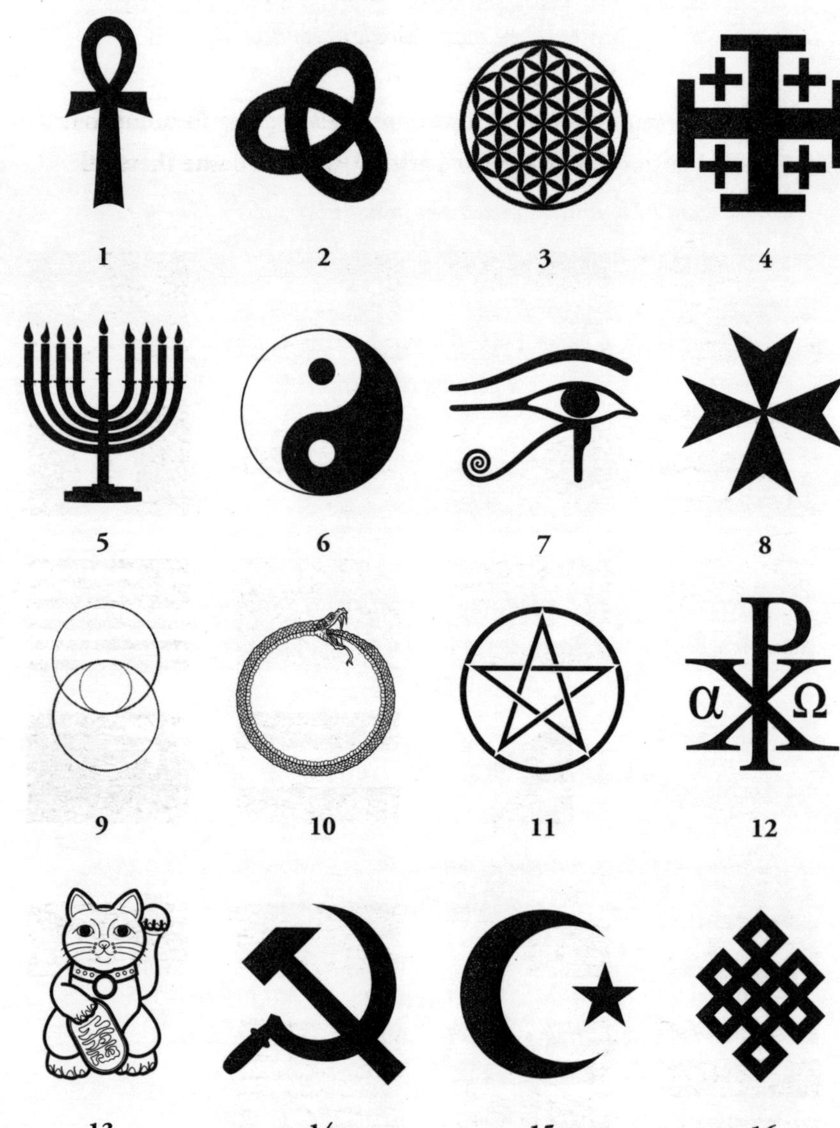

Answers on page 146

The Old Red, White and Blue

Think you know all the flags of the world? Well, here's a chance to prove it. There are 23 countries in the world whose flags are entirely red, white and blue.

Using the image below as a prompt, and bearing in mind that several nations have similar patterns can you name them all?

Answers on page 147

Lingua Franca

Can you name the 10 languages that are spoken by the most native speakers in the world?

According to number of speakers can you name the country or region where these languages are spoken?

1. **Pawnee**
2. **Xhosa**
3. **Koro**
4. **Hakka**
5. **Hausa**
6. **Tagalog**
7. **Khmer**
8. **Chittagonian**
9. **Kernowek**
10. **Brezhoneg**

Can you identify these languages:

Köszönöm

Dziękuję Ci

Asante

Teşekkür Ederim

Merci

Go Raibh Maith Agat

Ngiyabonga

Terima Kasih

Takk Skal Du Ha

Mahalo

Answers on page 147

The Golfing Greats

Can you name the 19 players who have won five or more separate classics tournaments?

1.

2.

3.

4.

5.

6.

7.

8.

9.

10.

11.

12.

13.

14.

15.

16.

17.

18.

19.

Answers on page 148

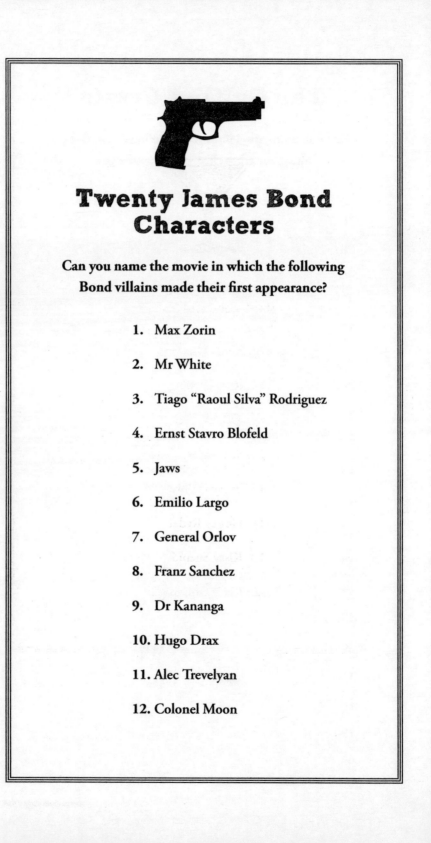

Twenty James Bond Characters

Can you name the movie in which the following Bond villains made their first appearance?

1. Max Zorin
2. Mr White
3. Tiago "Raoul Silva" Rodriguez
4. Ernst Stavro Blofeld
5. Jaws
6. Emilio Largo
7. General Orlov
8. Franz Sanchez
9. Dr Kananga
10. Hugo Drax
11. Alec Trevelyan
12. Colonel Moon

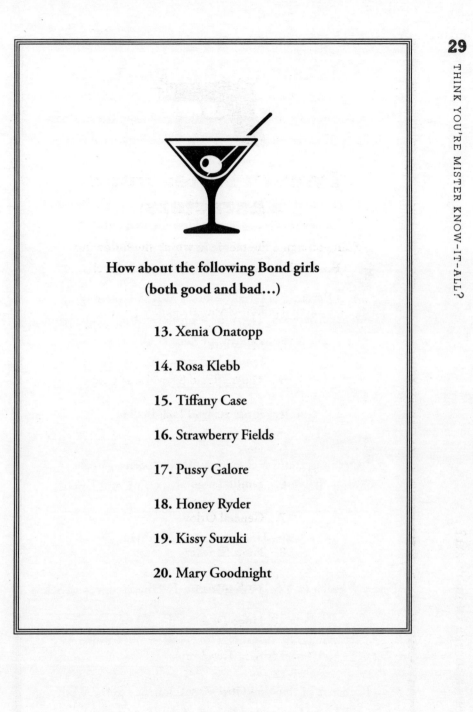

How about the following Bond girls (both good and bad…)

13. Xenia Onatopp

14. Rosa Klebb

15. Tiffany Case

16. Strawberry Fields

17. Pussy Galore

18. Honey Ryder

19. Kissy Suzuki

20. Mary Goodnight

Answers on page 149

Classical Conundrums

Test how familiar you are with ancient civilizations. What is the collective name for the following lists of names, activities or places:

Zeus, Hera, Poseidon, Demeter, Athena, Apollo, Artemis, Ares, Aphrodite, Hephaestus, Hermes, and either Hestia or Dionysus

____

Great Pyramid of Giza, Colossus of Rhodes, Hanging Gardens of Babylon, Lighthouse of Alexandria, Mausoleum at Halicarnassus, Statue of Zeus at Olympia, and Temple of Artemis

____

Aglaea, Euphrosyne, and Thalia

____

Oceanus, Tethys, Hyperion, Theia, Coeus, Phoebe, Cronus, Rhea, Mnemosyne, Themis, Crius, and Iapetus

____

Vespasian, Titus, and Domitian

____

Lever, Wheel and Axle, Pulley, Inclined Plane, Wedge, and Screw

____

Papermaking, Printing, Gunpowder, and Compass

____

Romance of the Three Kingdoms, Journey to the West, Water Margin, and Dream of the Red Chamber

Answers on page 149

Great Artworks

How much of a culture vulture are you? Do you know your Manet from your Monet and your Pollock from your Bacon? **Can you name the painters who created the following masterpieces?** The year of creation (which is sometimes an estimate) is included as a clue.

1. *Girl with a Pearl Earring*, 1665
2. *The Birth of Venus,* 1484–6
3. *The Starry Night*, 1889
4. *Arrangement in Grey and Black No. 1*, 1871
5. *The Kiss*, 1907–8
6. *The Arnolfini Portrait*, 1434
7. *The Garden of Earthly Delights*, 1503–15
8. *Self-Portrait with Thorn Necklace and Hummingbird,* 1940
9. *The Great Wave off Kanagawa*, 1829-33
10. *A Sunday Afternoon on the Island of La Grande Jatte*, 1884–86
11. *Les Demoiselles d'Avignon*, 1907
12. *The Harvesters*, 1565
13. *Le Déjeuner sur l'herbe*, 1863
14. *Composition with Red Blue and Yellow*, 1930
15. *The Naked Maja*, c. 1797–1800
16. *Wanderer above the Sea of Fog*, 1819
17. *Infinity Mirror Room, Phalli's Field,* 1965/2016
18. *Movement in Squares,* 1961
19. *The Raft of the Medusa*, 1818–19
20. *Nighthawks*, 1942
21. *Nude Descending a Staircase, No. 2*, 1912

Answers on pages 150

World's Great Tourist Attractions

Can you name the location of these tourist attractions around the world? One point for the country, one more for the city or location.

1. **Charles Bridge**
2. **Hagia Sophia**
3. **The Alhambra**
4. **Notre Dame Cathedral**
5. **Church of the Savior on Blood**
6. **Eiffel Tower**
7. **Golden Gate Bridge**
8. **Cristo Redentor**
9. **Alcatraz**
10. **St Peter's Basilica**
11. **Uluru**
12. **La Sagrada Familia**
13. **Sheikh Zayed Grand Mosque**
14. **Taj Mahal**
15. **Machu Picchu**
16. **Angkor Wat**
17. **Petronas Twin Towers**
18. **Chichen Itza**
19. **Wat Pho**
20. **The National September 11 Memorial**
21. **Burj Khalifa**
22. **Lincoln Memorial**

Six extra points if you can name which attraction was closed to the public in 2019

Answers on pages 150

Multiple Oscars

The following actors and actresses have won three or more acting Oscars (either for Best Actor/Actress or Best Supporting Actor/Actress). **How many of the movies they won them for can you name?**

For bonus points, name the year of the award.

Katharine Hepburn
Daniel Day-Lewis
Meryl Streep
Jack Nicholson
Ingrid Bergman
Walter Brennan

Answers on page 151

Oscars: Best International Feature Film

In the following years, the winner of this award went to a movie directed by the following directors. **Can you name the movie and the country that submitted it for consideration?**

1. 1949 Vittorio de Sica
2. 1951 Akira Kurosawa
3. 1956 Federico Fellini
4. 1958 Jacques Tati
5. 1960 Ingmar Bergman
6. 1967 Jiří Menzel
7. 1972 Luis Buñuel
8. 1979 Volker Schlöndorff
9. 1987 Gabriel Axel
10. 1989 Giuseppe Tornatore
11. 1993 Fernando Trueba
12. 1994 Nikita Mikhalkov
13. 1998 Roberto Benigni
14. 1999 Pedro Almodovar
15. 2000 Ang Lee
16. 2006 Florian Henckel von Donnersmarck
17. 2011 Asghar Farhadi
18. 2018 Alfonso Cuarón

Answers on page 151

History of Textiles

What is the source material for the following types of cloth:

Cotton
Silk
Angora wool
Cashmere wool
Piña
Rayon
Beta cloth

What was supposedly discovered by Leizu, wife of the Yellow Emperor, in the 27th century BC?

Who invented the first power loom, in 1784?

Who patented the cotton gin in 1793?

Who invented the spinning jenny?

Who invented the world's first successful sewing machine and when?

Name these embroidery stitches:

1.

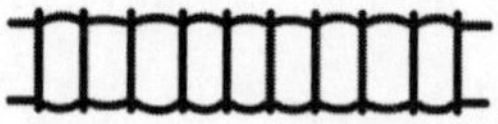

2.

3.

4.

5.

6.

Answers on page 152

Fictional Detectives

From Scandi Noir, to cosy crime and hardboiled detectives, crime fiction is popular around the world. **Can you name the authors who created each of these well-loved detectives in their fiction?**

Agatha Raisin

Aurelio Zen

Carl Mørck

Charlie Chan

Detective Galileo

Harry Hole

Inspector Montalbano

Inspector Morse

Inspector Rebus

Jackson Brodie

Kinsey Millhone

Kurt Wallander

Lisbeth Salander

Pepe Carvalho

Philip Marlowe

Piet Van der Valk

Precious Ramotswe

Stephanie Plum

Temperance Brennan

V.I. Warshawski

Answers on page 152

The Sequel

Here is a list of movies, some of which are good, some bad, and some plain ugly… All had sequels, and none of the titles were as obvious as to simply reuse the entire original title and shove a '2' on the end of it. How many of those sequels can you name (where more than one sequel was made, only the first gets a point).

1. *Pitch Black*
2. *Dirty Harry*
3. *The Ipcress File*
4. *Get Shorty*
5. *Donnie Darko*
6. *Batman Begins*
7. *Dumb and Dumber*
8. *Alvin and the Chipmunks*
9. *A Fish Called Wanda*
10. *Happiness*
11. *The Hustler*
12. *Chinatown*
13. *Terms of Endearment*
14. *The Maltese Falcon*
15. *Saturday Night Fever*
16. *Yojimbo*
17. *The Love Bug*
18. *The Rocky Horror Picture Show*
19. *El Mariachi*
20. *A Fistful of Dollars*

Answers on pages 153

Mammoth Animals

Everyone knows that the blue whale is the largest animal in the world but can you name:

1. **The World's Heaviest Insect**
2. **The Largest Living Amphibian**
3. **The World's Largest Bird**
4. **The Biggest Reptile**
5. **The Largest Living Fish**
6. **The Biggest Carnivore That Lives on Land**
7. **The Tallest Animal**
8. **The Largest Land Mammal**

Answers on page 153

Asian Capitals

Can you name the capital city of the following countries?

1. Afghanistan
2. Azerbaijan
3. Bangladesh
4. Bhutan
5. China
6. India
7. Iran
8. Iraq
9. Japan
10. Laos
11. Malaysia
12. Mongolia
13. Pakistan
14. Philippines
15. Saudi Arabia
16. South Korea
17. Sri Lanka
18. Syria
19. Tajikistan
20. Thailand
21. Tibet
22. Turkey
23. United Arab Emirates
24. Uzbekistan
25. Vietnam

Answers on page 153

Famous Philosophical Quotes

Here are some well-known quotes that encapsulate the beliefs of some of the world's great philosophers.
Do you know who said them?

'The unexamined life is not worth living.'

'Whereof one cannot speak, thereof one must be silent.'

'I think, therefore I am.' ('Cogito, ergo sum.')

'God is dead! He remains dead! And we have killed him.'

'Liberty consists in doing what one desires.'

'If God did not exist, it would be necessary to invent Him.'

'Philosophy is a battle against the bewitchment of our intelligence by means of language.'

'We are what we repeatedly do. Excellence, then, is not an act, but a habit.'

'The mind is furnished with ideas by experience alone.'

'Life must be understood backward. But it must be lived forward.'

'Is man merely a mistake of God's? Or God merely a mistake of man's?'

'Religion is the sign of the oppressed ... it is the opium of the people.'

'Happiness is the highest good.'

'If men were born free, they would, so long as they remained free, form no conception of good and evil.'

'Man is condemned to be free.'

'The only thing I know is that I know nothing.'

'Man is born free, but is everywhere in chains.'

'Happiness lies in virtuous activity, and perfect happiness lies in the best activity, which is contemplative.'

'To do as one would be done by, and to love one's neighbour as oneself, constitute the ideal perfection of utilitarian morality.'

'Everything that exists is born for no reason, carries on living through weakness, and dies by accident.'

Answers on pages 154

Dog Breeds

Can you name the breeds of dogs shown below?

Answers on page 154

Twenty Questions: The Birth of Social Media

How well do you know your online history? Social media is a relatively recent phenomenon: do you know the year in which the following notable events happened? (They are in chronological order, which may help):

1. Usenet was first established
2. AOL Instant Messenger was first available
3. Yahoo Messenger was launched
4. MSN Messenger was launched
5. MySpace first became a social networking site (as opposed to a file sharing site)
6. Skype was launched
7. Facebook was founded by Mark Zuckerberg, Eduardo Saverin, Dustin Moskovitz, and Chris Hughes, who were students at Harvard University
8. Bebo was launched
9. Twitter was first launched (and first became popular in Brazil and India in particular)
10. Facebook launched News Feed
11. Instagram was launched
12. Quora, the question and answer networking site, was launched
13. LinkedIn filed for an IPO and launched its first shares
14. Snapchat was launched
15. Facebook went public with a valuation of $104 billion
16. Tinder, the dating network, was launched
17. Vine was launched, on the way to acquiring 200 million users
18. Twitter announced it would no longer allow uploads of Vine clips
19. Time Inc. acquired MySpace, which had long since been surpassed as the most popular social network in the world
20. Yahoo! Messenger was shut down

Answers on page 155

World Cup Glory

How many of the goalscorers can you name from the following soccer World Cup finals? (Only goals scored in full time and extra time count, not penalty shoot-out goals.)

1958 | Brazil 5 Sweden 2

1962 | Brazil 3 Czechoslovakia 1

1966 | England 4 Germany 2

1970 | Brazil 4 Italy 1

1974 | West Germany 2 Netherlands 1

1978 | Argentina 3 Italy 1

1982 | Italy 3 West Germany 1

1986 | Argentina 3 West Germany 2

1990 | West Germany 1 Argentina 0

1994 | Brazil 0 Italy 0

1998 | France 3 Brazil 0

2002 | Brazil 2 Germany 0

2006 | France 1 Italy 1

2010 | Spain 1 Netherlands 0

2014 | Germany 1 Argentina 0

2018 | France 4 Croatia 2

Answers on page 156

States of the Union

Looking at the diagram below, how many US states can you name?

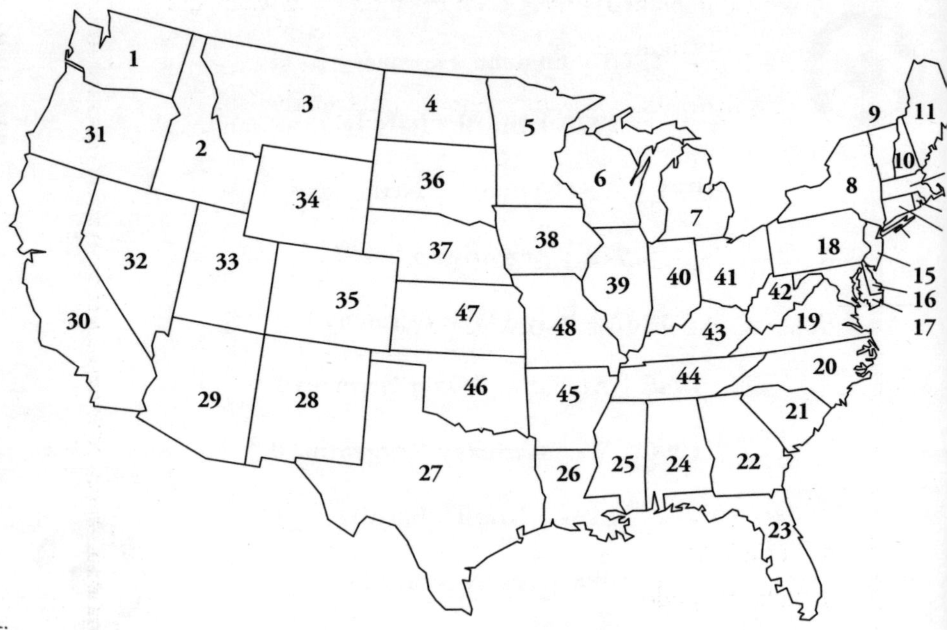

Which states are missing from the image?

How many of the state capitals can you name?

Answers on pages 157

Twenty Questions: Musical Moments

1. What is the difference between a symphony and a concerto?
2. What order do the movements of a concerto have to come in?
3. Why is an orchestra called a Philharmonic and where did the term originate?
4. How many different white musical notes are there in a piano octave?
5. Name the four instruments in a standard string quartet
6. What is an a cappella piece of music?

What do these musical terms mean?

7. Adagio
8. Allegro
9. Fortissimo
10. Berceuse
11. Cadence
12. Diminuendo
13. Ostinato
14. Octet

Name the following musical symbols:

15. 16. 17. 18. 19. 20.

Answers on page 159

Platonic Solids

The Platonic solids are regular polyhedrons – solids whose identical faces all have edges the same length as well as the same number of faces meeting at each corner.

There are only five such shapes, all pictured below.
Can you label them correctly?

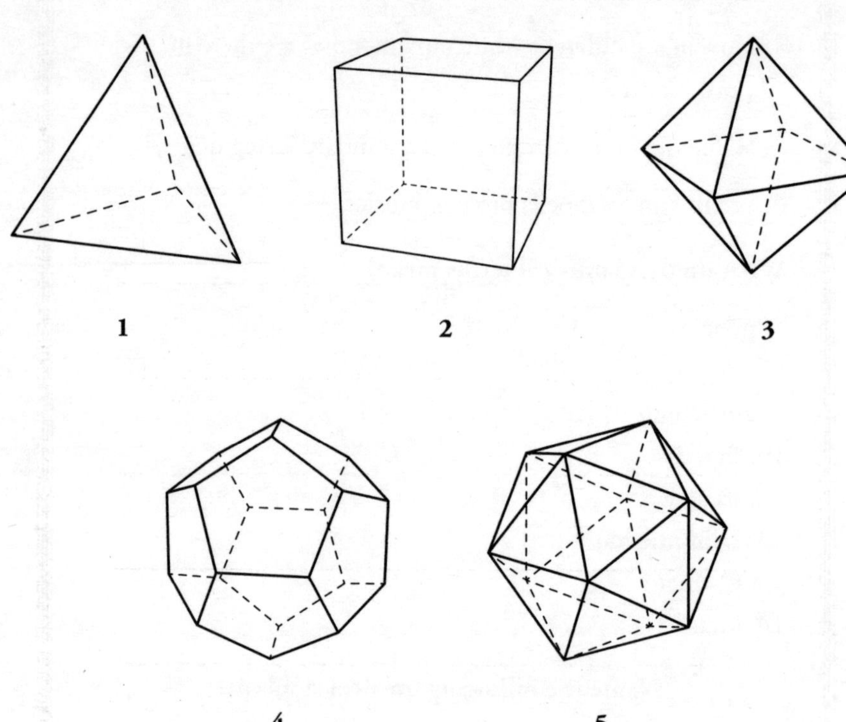

Answers on pages 160

Prime Numbers

The prime numbers, starting 2, 3, 5, 7… whose only whole factors are 1 and themselves.

How quickly can you name all the primes under 100?

Answers on page 160

Capital Cities of South America

Which countries are these cities the capitals of?

1. **Asuncion**
2. **Bogota**
3. **Brasilia**
4. **Buenos Aires**
5. **Caracas**
6. **Georgetown**
7. **Lima**
8. **Montevideo**
9. **Quito**
10. **Santiago**

Answers on page 160

Strange Currencies

They say money makes the world go round… Here is a list of the standard three capital letter abbreviations for currencies of the world: can you give the correct currency name and country for each? For instance, for USD, the answer would be: US dollar, United States of America.

AFN	INR
ARS	IQD
AUD	JPY
BBD	KES
BGN	KRW
BOB	LBP
BRL	MXN
CAD	MYR
CHF	NOK
CNY	NZD
COP	PKR
DKK	PLN
EGP	RSD
GEL	RUB
HRK	SAR
HTG	TRY
HUF	VND
ILS	ZAR

Answers on page 160

K-Pop Hits

K-Pop is the genre of pop music that originated in South Korea in the 1990s but which has become a huge global phenomenon since the 2000s, as millions of youthful fans around the world have followed the bands via social media and the internet.

Can you name any (or all) of the Top 10 K-Pop bands according to Tumblr in 2019?

1.

2.

3.

4.

5.

6.

7.

8.

9.

10.

Answers on pages 161

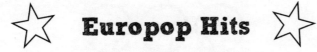

Europop Hits

If your musical memory goes back further, can you name the year of release of the following Europop hits that were popular around the world?

(Don't try to remember the tunes though… Some of them are likely to get stuck in your head for days, and it won't necessarily be for a good reason.)

2 Unlimited, 'There's No Limit'

Rednex, 'Cotton Eye Joe'

Boney M, 'Rasputin'

Roxette, 'Joyride'

Abba, 'Waterloo'

Snap!, 'The Power'

Ace of Base, 'All That She Wants'

Haddaway, 'What is Love?'

Aqua, 'Barbie Girl'

Army of Lovers, 'Crucified'

Vengaboys, 'Boom, Boom, Boom, Boom'

Answers on page 161

Summer Olympic Sports

Below is a list that includes the 33 current summer sports (Tokyo 2021) along with nine discontinued sports.
Can you spot the nine that have been discontinued?

Aquatics
Archery
Athletics
Badminton
Baseball/Softball
Basketball
Boxing
Canoe/Kayak
Cricket
Croquet
Cycling
Equestrian
Fencing
Field hockey
Football
Golf
Gymnastics
Handball
Jeu de Paume
Judo
Karate

Lacrosse
Modern pentathlon
Motor boating
Pelota
Polo
Roque racket
Rowing
Rugby sevens
Sailing
Shooting
Skateboarding
Sport climbing
Surfing
Table tennis
Tae kwon do
Tennis
Triathlon
Tug of war
Volleyball
Weightlifting
Wrestling

Answers on page 161

Name the Author

Can you name the author of the following acclaimed novels from around the world:

1. *The Wind-Up Bird Chronicle*
2. *2666*
3. *Beloved*
4. *The Edible Woman*
5. *Atomised*
6. *The Tin Drum*
7. *The White Tiger*
8. *Love in the Time of Cholera*
9. *Invisible Man*
10. *The Kite Runner*
11. *The Kitchen God's Wife*
12. *Oscar and Lucinda*
13. *Things Fall Apart*
14. *Sophie's Choice*
15. *The Sound and the Fury*
16. *1984*
17. *Dream of Ding Village*
18. *The Golden Notebook*
19. *The Master and Margarita*

How many of the 21st century's winners of the Nobel Prize for Literature can you name? (If you're a literature geek, shame on you if you miss any. For more casual readers, the more you can name the more kudos you get.)

Answers on page 162

What's in a Name?

What were the names of the following countries before their most recent change of name?

Eswatini
Congo
Myanmar
Burkina Faso
Cambodia
Benin
Transjordan
Iran
North Macedonia
Namibia
Ghana
Mali
Thailand
Indonesia
Bangladesh
Tuvalu
Saudi Arabia
Mexico
Vanuatu
Belize
Lesotho
Ireland
Iraq
Kiribati
Malawi

Answers on page 162

Colour

My daughter once asked me if everything was in black and white when I was a child... Unfortunately that wasn't true, but the world of colour really is evolving in the digital age: now even the newspapers are in colour. Can you answer these colour-based posers?

1. Can you name the three primary colours?

2. What are their complementary colours (also known as the secondary colours)?

3. Which three colours does the human eye perceive?

4. What are the four colours used in CMYK printing?

5. Just for fun, what do you think this list of colours might be?

Cerulean, Fuchsia Rose, True Red, Aqua Sky, Tigerlily, Blue Turquoise, Sand Dollar, Chili Pepper, Blue Iris, Mimosa, Turquoise, Honeysuckle, Tangerine Tango, Emerald, Radiant Orchid, Marsala, Rose Quartz, Serenity, Greenery, Ultra Violet, Living Coral

6. What colours do the following substances produce when they are used as natural dyes?

Cochineal insect
Cow urine
Lac insect red
Murex snail
Catechu or Cutch tree
Himalayan rhubarb root
Indigofera plant
Kamala tree
Larkspur plant

7. What colour are these gemstones?

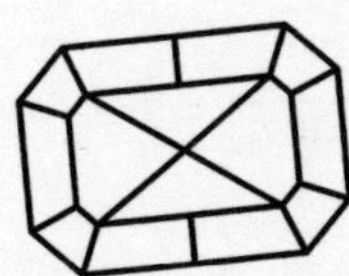

Lapiz lazuli
Ruby
Peridot
Tanzanite
Emerald

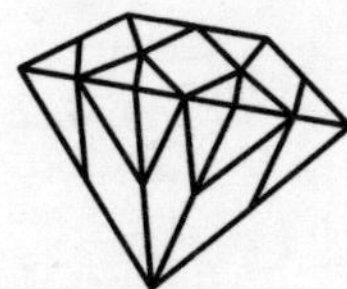

Answers on page 163

Mixing up the Elements

As you probably know, given that you are a Mr or Ms Know-It-All, water (H_20) is a compound of hydrogen and oxygen.

1. Without giving the chemical formulae, can you name the elements which make up the following common compounds?

1. Salt	5. Marble
2. Bronze	6. Laughing gas
3. Ammonia	7. Baking soda
4. Sand	8. Steel

2. Can you name the first ten elements and their chemical symbols?

3. Can you correctly label the diagram of an atom below?

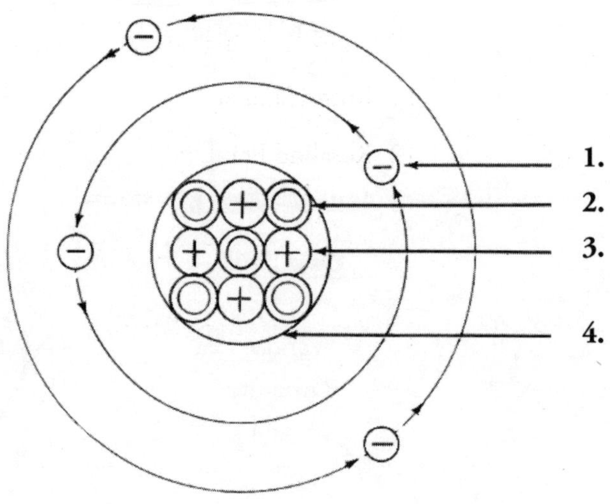

Answers on page 163

Female Inventors and Discoverers

Can you name the most notable invention or discovery of the following renowned inventors, scientists and entrepreneurs?

1. Joy Mangano
2. Ada Lovelace
3. Elizabeth J. Magie
4. Marie Curie
5. Melitta Bentz
6. Caresse Crosby
7. Ruth Graves Wakefield
8. Grace Hopper
9. Maria Goeppert-Mayer
10. Dorothy Hodgkin
11. Ruth Handler
12. Rosalind Franklin
13. Stephanie Kwolek
14. Jane Goodall
15. Patsy O'Connell Sherman

Answers on page 164

The Movies of Richard Curtis

British director Richard Curtis has worked as either writer or director on thirteen movies.

Can you name them all?

1.

2.

3.

4.

5.

6.

7.

8.

9.

10.

11.

12.

13.

Answers on page 164

The Wizard of Oz Trivia

Can you name the actors who played the characters below?

1. Dorothy Gale
2. Professor Marvel/The Wizard of Oz/Emerald City Doorman/the Cabby/Emerald City Guard
3. 'Hunk' / Scarecrow
4. 'Hickory' / Tin Man
5. 'Zeke' / the Cowardly Lion
6. Glinda
7. Miss Almira Gulch / The Wicked Witch of the West
8. Auntie Em
9. Toto
10. The actor who played the scarecrow was original cast as the Tin Man but they swapped roles before production began. The actor he swapped with then had a serious allergic reaction to the Tin Man's make-up and had to be replaced. Can you name that actor?
11. What colour were Dorothy's shoes in the original book?
12. Can you name the author of the original book?

Answers on page 165

The Games Compendium

Can you name the six chess pieces depicted below?

Can you rank all poker winning hands from high to low?

Can you place the 15 black and 15 white backgammon pieces on this board, ready for a game?

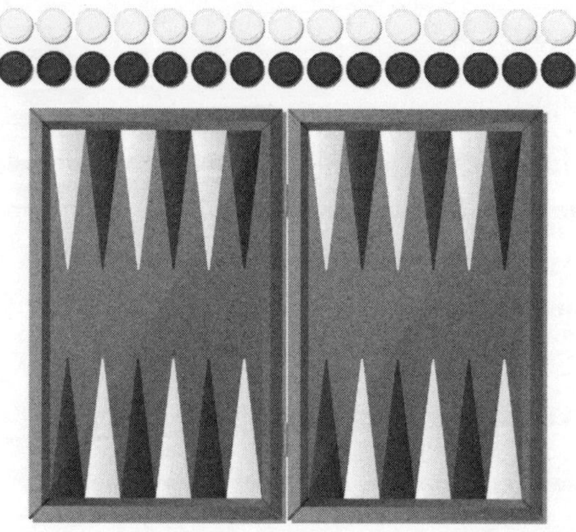

The balls on a snooker table have values ranging from 1 to 7.
Can you name all the colours in the correct order?

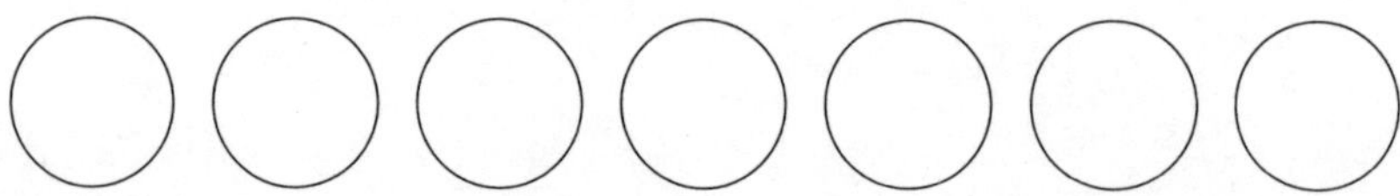

Answers on page 165

All the Sevens

There's something special about the number seven: the alchemists saw it as magical, which is why Isaac Newton (who dabbled in the alchemical arts) decided the rainbow had to have seven colours…

Can you name:

The Seven Virtues

The Seven Dwarves

The Magnificent Seven (the actors in the 1960 version)

The Seven Sins

The Seven Seas (or Oceans)

The Seven Colours of the Rainbow

The Seven Hills of Rome

The Seven Metals of Antiquity

Answers on page 166

Which Continent?

Here is a list of the tallest mountains from each continent of the world. **Can you name the correct continent for each one?**

Mount Everest
Aconcagua
Mount McKinley
Mount Kilimanjaro
Mount Elbrus
Vinson Massif
Mount Kosciusko

What is the longest river in each of these six continents?
(Australia is given to avoid possible confusions over the answer…)

Africa
Asia
Australia
Europe
North America
South America

Answers on page 167

The Long and Short of It

There is a divide in the world between those who use the metric and imperial systems. And beyond that, it is important to know your centi- from your milli- and your miles from your nautical miles.

How many of the following conversions can you perform?
For the first ten questions, only exact answers will do. For the second ten, a close guess gets a point (we've given answers to two decimal places, where appropriate).

1. **How many litres in a cubic metre?**
2. **How many feet are there in a mile?**
3. **How many micrometres in a millimetre?**
4. **How many ounces are there in a pound?**
5. **A car is travelling at 1,000 metres per minute. What is its speed in kilometres per hour?**
6. **How many metres squared in a hectare?**
7. **How many leap years are there in 400 years?**
8. **How many minutes in a week?**
9. **How many pounds in an imperial ton? (Hint: a North American 'short ton' is 2,000 pounds).**
10. **How many centigrams in a kilogram?**
11. **How many inches are there in a kilometre?**
12. **How many millimetres in a foot?**
13. **How many square feet in a square metre?**
14. **How many hours are there in a lunar month?**
15. **How many ounces in 100 grams?**
16. **How many miles in a nautical mile?**
17. **How many nautical miles per hour is a knot?**
18. **How many cubic feet per minute in one litre per second?**
19. **How many ounces in a kilogram?**
20. **How many miles in a light year?**

Answers on page 167

The Classical Orchestra

The classical era of orchestral music is generally reckoned to be the second half of the 18th century, when two of the most talented composers at work were Mozart and Haydn. In this period the classical orchestra had a standardized line-up that is often recreated today.

How many of the instruments can you name?

Can you name the composer of the following major pieces of classical music:

1. **Peer Gynt**
2. **The Four Seasons**
3. **Ride of the Valkyries**
4. **The Planets**
5. **Clair de Lune** (from Suite bergamasque)
6. **Brandenburg Concertos**
7. **Swan Lake**
8. **Gymnopédie No. 1**
9. **Pomp and Circumstance**
10. **Carmen**
11. **The Magic Flute**
12. **Moonlight Sonata**

Answers on page 168

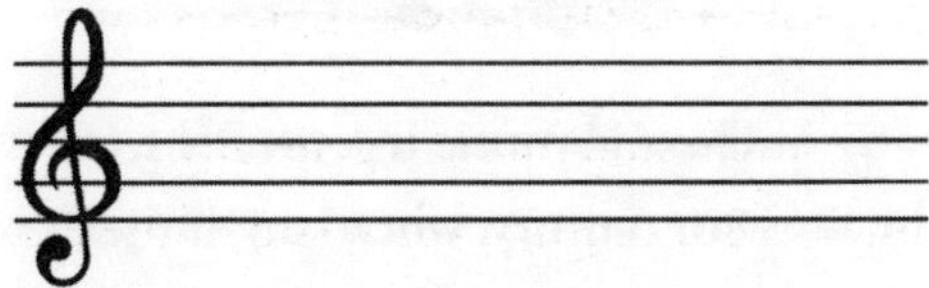

Musical Modes

Can you name the seven musical modes used in early Western music?

1.

2.

3.

4.

5.

6.

7.

Answers on page 168

Classic Plays

For how many of these classic plays running from antiquity up to the modern day can you name the playwright:

THE ANCIENTS

Oedipus the King

The Frogs

The Brothers Menaechmus

16TH AND 17TH CENTURIES

Edward II

Twelfth Night

The Alchemist

The White Devil

Fuenteovejuna

Life Is a Dream

The Misanthrope

Andromache

The Rover

Venice Preserv'd

18TH AND 19TH CENTURIES

The Servant of Two Masters
She Stoops to Conquer
The School for Scandal
The Marriage of Figaro
Don Carlos
The Broken Jug
The Wild Duck
The Power of Darkness
The Father
Spring Awakening
The Importance of Being Earnest
Uncle Vanya

20TH AND 21ST CENTURIES

Peter Pan
Pygmalion
Exiles
Juno and the Paycock
The Front Page
Machinal
Design for Living
The House of Bernarda Alba
The Life of Galileo
Long Day's Journey into Night
A Streetcar Named Desire
The Chairs
The Deep Blue Sea
The Crucible
The Caretaker
Absurd Person Singular
Death and the King's Horseman
Dancing at Lughnasa
The Goat

Answers on page 168

Dem Bones

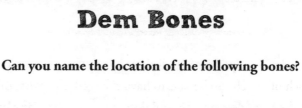

Can you name the location of the following bones?

Cervical vertebrae
Trapezium
Calcaneus
Navicular bone
Malleus
Humerus
Maxillae
Clavicles
Ulna
Metatarsals
Zygomatic bone
Lacrimal bone
Scaphoid bone
Coccygeal vertebrae
Vomer
Occipital bone
Femur
Temporal bones
Patella
Intermediate phalanges

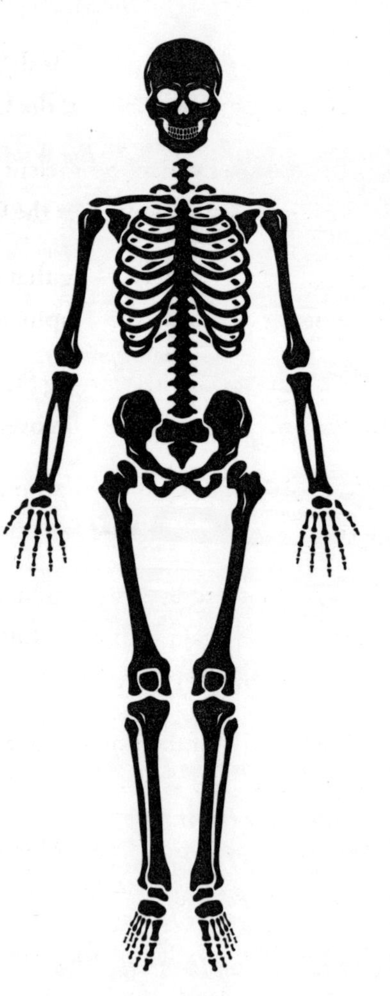

Answers on page 170

Great Battles of the World

Here is a brief description of 20 decisive battles from the history of the world, each of which can be said to have changed the course of history.

From the brief description and date, can you name the battle?

1. **A Greek army based in Athens defeated the greater Persian force, leading to a turning point in the Greco-Persian Wars, 490 BC**
2. **The battle after which the ancient Persian empire came under the subjugation of Alexander the Great, 331 BC**
3. **The attempted river crossing that ended Alexander the Great's attempt at expanding his empire into India, 326 BC**
4. **The battle during the Warring States period in China which led to the final victory of the Qin over the Zhao, 262 BC**
5. **The decisive victory in the Second Punic War between Rome and Carthage, in which Rome gained the upper hand, 207 BC**
6. **The Teutons, led by Arminius, defeated the Romans under Varusi: never again would the Romans succeed in expanding to the east of the Rhine, AD 9**
7. **A final victory of the Romans over the Huns, driving Attila back at great cost, AD 451**
8. **The victory won by Charles Martel which pushed back and prevented any further Arab conquest of Western Europe, AD 732**
9. **The battle in which a raiding party from northern France took power in England, 1066**
10. **Joan of Arc's victory over the English, which probably ended any chance of France becoming an English dominion, 1429**

Answers on page 170

11. The sea battle in which England defended itself against a naval force from a major European power of the day, 1588

12. A major battle that preserved Vienna from an advancing French and Bavarian force, 1704

13. The battle won by Peter the Great which led to the decline of the powerful Swedish empire and the rise of Russia as a European power, 1709

14. Fought in New York State, the decisive victory of the American Revolutionary War which led to the surrender of the British under Burgoyne, 1777

15. The first major military victory by the French Army following the French Revolution, 1792

16. The battle that marked the end of the Napoleonic Wars, 1815

17. The battle often described as the turning point of the American Civil War, in which Maj. Gen. George Meade's Army of the Potomac defeated attacks by Confederate Gen. Robert E. Lee's Army of Northern Virginia, July 1863

18. The deadliest battle of World War One in which more than a million people were killed or wounded, July-Nov 1916

19. The decisive battle of the Desert War in which the forces led by Montgomery defeated those led by Rommel, October 1942

20. A crucial turning point during the British and Allied forces fight against Japanese forces in north-eastern India, March-July 1944

Exploring the Universe

Here is a list of space flights and probes (and the date of launch) that we have sent out into the universe on a voyage of discovery and exploration.

Can you say which star, planet or moon (or other object) was the destination of each?

1. Mariner 10, 1973
2. Spirit, 2003
3. Cassini-Huygens, 1997
4. Mangalayaan, 2013
5. MESSENGER, 2004
6. Venera 4, 1967
7. InSight, 2018
8. Dawn, 2017
9. Pioneer 10, 1972
10. IKAROS, 2010
11. Mariner 6, 1969
12. New Horizons, 2006
13. Voyager 2, 1977
14. Giotto, 1985
15. Ranger 7, 1964
16. Galileo, 1989
17. Sojourner, 1996
18. Cassini, 1998
19. Viking 1 Orbiter, 1976
20. Apollo 11, 1969
21. Parker Solar Probe, 2018
22. Surveyor 1, 1966
23. Gaia, 2013

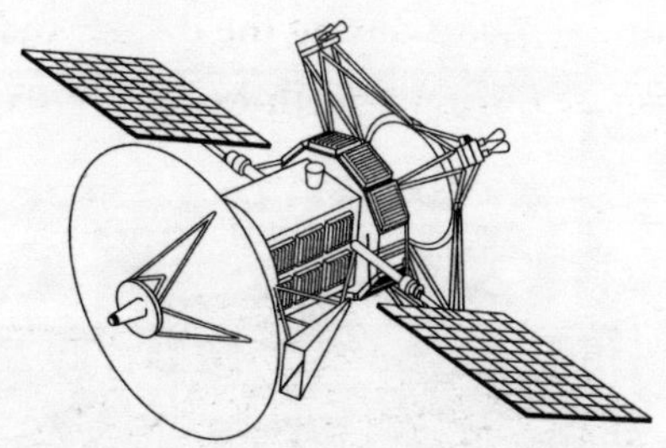

Answers on page 171

Hit Songs

At the time of writing there are 15 singles that have sold 15 million or more copies worldwide.

Here are the artists and years of release: can you name the songs?

1. Bing Crosby, 1942
2. Elton John, 1997
3. Mungo Jerry, 1970
4. Bing Crosby, 1935
5. Bill Haley & His Comets, 1954
6. Whitney Houston, 1992
7. Elvis Presley, 1960
8. USA for Africa, 1985
9. The Ink Spots,1939
10. Baccara, 1977
11. Celine Dion, 1997
12. Mariah Carey, 1994
13. Bryan Adams, 1991
14. John Travolta and Olivia Newton-John, 1978
15. Scorpions, 1991

These songs have sold between 10 and 15 million copies.

Can you name the artists for each song?

1. 'I Will Survive', 1978
2. 'Sweet Mother', 1976
3. 'Sukiyaki', 1963
4. 'Da Da Da', 1982
5. 'Rudolph the Red-Nosed Reindeer', 1949
6. 'I Want to Hold Your Hand', 1963
7. 'Time to Say Goodbye', 1996
8. 'Y.M.C.A.', 1978
9. 'Do They Know It's Christmas?', 1984
10. 'Believe', 1998
11. 'Kung Fu Fighting', 1974
12. 'Rock Your Baby', 1974
13. 'Paper Doll', 1943
14. 'The Last Farewell', 1975
15. 'Fernando', 1976
16. 'Wabash Cannonball', 1942
17. 'Diana', 1957
18. 'Un-Break My Heart', 1996
19. 'My Sweet Lord', 1970
20. 'Macarena', 1995
21. 'Chirpy Chirpy Cheep Cheep', 1971
22. 'I'm a Believer', 1966
23. 'Mundian To Bach Ke', 1998
24. 'Tennessee Waltz', 1950
25. 'Earth Angel', 1954
26. 'Hound Dog', 1956
27. 'A Whiter Shade of Pale', 1967
28. '...Baby One More Time', 1998

Answers on page 172

Space Firsts

How many of the following can you identify by name?

1957 – First Satellite to Orbit Earth

1957 – First Animal in Space

1961 – First Human in Space

1961 – First American in Space

1962 – First American to Orbit the Earth

1963 – First Woman in Space

1965 – First Space Walk Cosmonaut

1967 – First Person to Die in Space

1969 – First Man on the Moon

1970 – First Space Rescue (name of craft)

1972 – First Spacecraft to Leave the Solar System

1973 – First American Space Station

1976 – First Mars Landing

1981 – First Reusable Space Vehicle

1984 – First Untethered Space Walk

1986 – First Civilian Death

1990 – First Space Telescope

2001 – First Space Tourist

2003 – First Person to Be Married from Space

2004 – First Spacecraft to Orbit Saturn

Answers on page 173

The Tennis Greats

As of 2019, there are 14 men's tennis players who have won five or more grand slam singles titles in the open era (which started in 1968). **How many of them can you name?**

There are six male players in the open era who have won three or more grand slams in the same year. **Can you name them?**

And to this day, only two men have won all four grand slam titles in a single calendar year. Both are from before the open era. **Can you name them?**

And as of 2019 there are 12 women's tennis players who have won five or more grand slam singles titles in the open era. **Can you name them?**

There are six female players in the open era who have won three or more grand slams in the same year. **Can you name them?**

And there are three female players who have won all four grand slams in one calendar year. Two were in the open era and one was earlier. **Can you name all three?**

Answers on page 173

International Co-operation

Can you identify which international organization each of these logos belongs to?

1

2

3

4

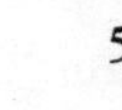

5

6

7

8

9

10

11

12

Answers on page 175

Which Wedding Anniversary?

Here is a list of the traditional wedding anniversary gifts for the first 10 years of married life and then for the 15th, 20th, 25th, 30th, 40th, 50th and 60th years.

Can you correctly add the number of years to each item in the list?

Ruby
Iron
Diamond
Paper
Pearl
Wool/Copper
Bronze
Crystal
Cotton
China
Golden
Tin /Aluminium
Leather
Linen/Silk
Wood
Silver
Pottery

Answers on page 175

Twenty Traditional Costumes

Can you name at least one country in which each of the following costumes or items of clothing is the traditional way of dressing?

Sari

Chut

Pollera

Huaso Attire

Abaya and Thobe

Gomesi

Þjóðbúningur karla

Kimono

Kebaya

Bunad

Hanbok

Zhongshan suit

Lederhosen

Shúkà

Kilt

Dhoti and Lungi

Sarafan

Agbada

Bamileke Elephant Mask

Huipil

Answers on page 176

Russia's Neighbours

Russia's land border is approximately 12,577 miles long, which is the world's second-longest. It has land borders with 14 countries which are recognized by most international bodies.
Can you name them?

Russia also has borders with two countries whose sovereignty is not universally recognized. **Can you name them?**

Which of Russia's land borders is the longest?

Which country is the only one to have a longer land border than Russia?

What are the longest single land borders in the northern and southern hemispheres?

Answers on page 176

Mythical Hybrids

The following are all mythical creatures from around the world which take their features from more than one animal, so are hybrids. For each can you name two creatures which their features come from?

	Jackalope	
	Selkie	
	Myrmecoleon	
	Chamrosh	
	Zu	
	Minotaur	
	Allocamelus	
	Lycanthrope	
	Faun	
	Cockatrice	
	Centaur	
	Longma	
	Merlion	
	Kishi	
	Yeren	
	Al-mi'raj	

Answers on page 177

Classical Mythology

Here is a list of Greek gods and goddesses. For each, can you name their role or say what they were the god or goddess of?

Aphrodite
Ares
Artemis
Athena
Demeter
Dionysus
Hades
Hephaestus
Hermes
Poseidon
Tyche

In Roman mythology, who do these descriptions match up to?

King of the gods; son of Saturn, god of sky and thunder; patron god of Rome

Queen of the gods; wife and sister of Jupiter, daughter of Saturn, patron goddess of Rome

Goddess of wisdom, arts, trade and strategy

God of freshwater and the sea

Goddess of love

God of war

God of music, healing, light and truth

Goddess of the hunt, birth and the moon

God of fire and the forge

Goddess of hearth, home and family

God of profit and trade, who guided dead souls to the underworld

Goddess of agriculture, grain and marriage

Answers on page 177

Geological Time Periods

When classifying rocks and fossils, scientists split time up into the following set of periods.

Can you put them into the correct order? The list of dates on the right may help, each time period matches up to one of the periods mentioned.

Jurassic	570–510 million years ago
Silurian	510–439 million years ago
Pleistocene	439–409 million years ago
Eocene	409–363 million years ago
Ordovician	363–290 million years ago
Carboniferous	290–245 million years ago
Cambrian	245–208 million years ago
Permian	208–146 million years ago
Miocene	146–65 million years ago
Pliocene	65–56.5 million years ago
Palaeocene	56.5–35.4 million years ago
Devonian	35.4–23.3 million years ago
Holocene	23.3–5.2 million years ago
Triassic	5.2–2.5 million years ago
Cretaceous	2.5 million–12,000 years ago
Oligocene	12,000 years ago–present day

Answers on page 178

Dinosaur Names

The British scientist Richard Owen came up with the name for dinosaurs, which means 'terrible lizard'. Most dinosaurs' names are derived from Latin words.

Can you work out what the meaning of the following names is?

1. **Stegosaurus**
2. **Triceratops**
3. **Tyrannosaurus**
4. **Velociraptor**
5. **Apatosaurus**
6. **Diplodocus**
7. **Iguanodon**
8. **Brachiosaurus**
9. **Gigantosaurus**
10. **Seismosaurus**
11. **Spinosaurus**
12. **Ankylosaurus**
13. **Giraffatitan**
14. **Lesothosaurus**
15. **Saurolophus**

Answers on page 178

Highest Grossing Movies by Year

Can you name the highest grossing movies for each year of the 21st century?

This is much trickier, but how many of the highest grossing movies for the last 50 years of the 20th century can you name? Note that for some of these years there are two or three movies that could be counted as highest grossing according to different measures, so there is more than one answer that can be counted as correct.

Finally, the *Guinness Book of Records* gives an inflation-adjusted list of the top 10 grossing movies of all time. **How many of the top 10 can you guess?**

Answers on page 179

A Cornucopia of Villainy

Can you name the authors who originally created the following fictional villains or anti-heroes and the name of the books, stories or plays they first appeared in?

1. Mr Hyde
2. Professor Moriarty
3. Mrs Danvers
4. Uriah Heep
5. Cathy Ames
6. Heathcliff
7. Dr Frankenstein
8. Hannibal Lecter
9. David Melrose
10. Nils Bjurman
11. Tom Ripley
12. Nurse Ratched
13. Simon Legree
14. Norman Bates
15. O'Brien
16. Cruella De Vil
17. Patrick Bateman
18. Humbert Humbert
19. Sauron
20. Annie Wilkes
21. Milo Minderbinder
22. Iago
23. Alec D'Urberville
24. Svidrigailov

Answers on page 182

Twenty Questions: Biology

When classifying species, 'Species' is the most precise level of eight taxonomic ranks. **Can you name the other seven?**

There are three main branches of biology.
Name the branches that study:
Plants
Animals
Microorganisms

Can you name the six kingdoms of life?

Just four elements constitute about 96% of every living cell in existence. **What are the four elements?**

Answers on page 183

The Movies of Daniel Day-Lewis

Sometimes referred to as the world's greatest actor, Day-Lewis has appeared in just 20 movies.

Can you name them?

1.
2.
3.
4.
5.
6.
7.
8.
9.
10.
11.
12.
13.
14.
15.
16.
17.
18.
19.
20.

In addition, he appeared in one uncredited role.

Can you name the movie?

Answers on page 183

Chinese Dynasties

Can you rearrange this list of the dynasties, historical periods and rulers of China into the correct order? The list of dates on the right may give you some clues; each matches up to one of the periods listed.

Xia (Hsia)	2205–1766 BC
Southern and Northern	1766–1122 BC
Sui	1122–770 BC
Tang	770–476 BC
Han	476 – 221 BC
Spring & Autumn Annals	221–206 BC
Qin (Chin)	206 BC–AD 220
Three Kingdoms	AD 220–265
People's Republic of China	AD 265–420
Five Dynasties	AD 420–580
Shang	AD 589–618
Ming	AD 618–907
Jin (Tsin)	AD 907–960
Warring States	960–1280
Republic of China	1280–1368
Zhou (Chow)	1368–1644
Song (Sung)	1644–1911
Qing (Ching)	1911–1949
Yuan	1949–present

Answers on page 184

North to South

Here is a list of cities of the world. **Can you place them in the correct order from north to south by latitude?**

Aberdeen, Scotland

Auckland, New Zealand

Beijing, China

Berlin, Germany

Brisbane, Australia

Cairo, Egypt

Cape Town, South Africa

Darwin, Australia

Helsinki, Finland

Hobart, Tasmania

Jakarta, Indonesia

Kinshasa, Congo

Kuala Lumpur, Malaysia

Lisbon, Portugal

Manchester, England

Manila, Philippines

Mecca, Saudi Arabia

Mexico City, Mexico

Milan, Italy

Moscow, Russia

Oslo, Norway

Panama City, Panama

Paris, France

Perth, Australia

Rangoon, Myanmar

Reykjavík, Iceland

Rio de Janeiro, Brazil

Rome, Italy

Shanghai, China

Singapore, Singapore

Sydney, Australia

Tokyo, Japan

Wellington, New Zealand

Zürich, Switzerland

Answers on page 184

Time Zones

Now, let's go the other way around the world: time zones approximately match up to longitude rather than latitude. If it is noon in Times Square in New York, **what time is it in each of the following places?**

(Two points for the exact answer, one point if you are only an hour out as there is some variation through the year for some locations.)

Amsterdam, Netherlands

Athens, Greece

Bangkok, Thailand

Beijing, China

Berlin, Germany

Birmingham, England

Buenos Aires, Argentina

Cairo, Egypt

Cape Town, South Africa

Helsinki, Finland

Jakarta, Indonesia

Madrid, Spain

Mecca, Saudi Arabia

Mexico City, Mexico

Nairobi, Kenya

Odessa, Ukraine

Rio de Janeiro, Brazil

Rome, Italy

Shanghai, China

Stockholm, Sweden

Tripoli, Libya

Vladivostok, Russia

Wellington, New Zealand

Answers on page 185

The Albums of Bob Dylan

One of the true greats of rock and folk music, Bob Dylan has made 38 studio albums. **How many of them can you name?**

1.
2.
3.
4.
5.
6.
7.
8.
9.
10.
11.
12.
13.
14.
15.
16.
17.
18.
19.
20.
21.
22.
23.
24.
25.
26.
27.
28.
29.
30.
31.
32.
33.
34.
35.
36.
37.
38.

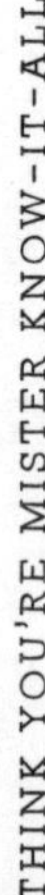

Answers on page 186

Presidents of the USA

There were 18 presidents of the United States of America in the 20th century.

Can you name them all in the correct order?

1.	**10.**
2.	**11.**
3.	**12.**
4.	**13.**
5.	**14.**
6.	**15.**
7.	**16.**
8.	**17.**
9.	**18.**

Can you also name the first five presidents after the Declaration of Independence?

And what about the 20th century's vice-presidents?

Answers on page 187

The Movies of Meryl Streep

A true grand dame of modern cinema, Meryl Streep has appeared in 65 movies including one uncredited cameo.

How many of them can you name, and can you name the uncredited cameo?

1.	**23.**	**45.**
2.	**24.**	**46.**
3.	**25.**	**47.**
4.	**26.**	**48.**
5.	**27.**	**49.**
6.	**28.**	**50.**
7.	**29.**	**51.**
8.	**30.**	**52.**
9.	**31.**	**53.**
10.	**32.**	**54.**
11.	**33.**	**55.**
12.	**34.**	**56.**
13.	**35.**	**57.**
14.	**36.**	**58.**
15.	**37.**	**59.**
16.	**38.**	**60.**
17.	**39.**	**61.**
18.	**40.**	**62.**
19.	**41.**	**63.**
20.	**42.**	**64.**
21.	**43.**	**65.**
22.	**44.**	

Answers on page 188

More Than Landlocked

Depending on which countries you count (as some are unrecognized by international organizations) there are 49 countries in the world which don't have a coastal border, meaning they are landlocked. Most are landlocked by three or more other countries. However, there are a few exceptions.

Seven internationally recognized countries are landlocked by just two countries. **Can you name them, and the two countries that surround them?**

Three countries are enclaves, meaning they are entirely surrounded by a single country. **Can you name them?**

Finally, there are two countries that are double landlocked. This means that they are landlocked by countries which are themselves landlocked. **Can you name them? And how many of their neighbours can you name?**

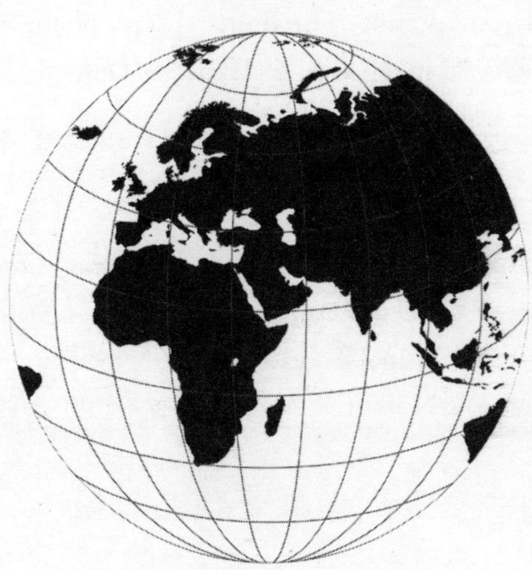

Answers on page 189

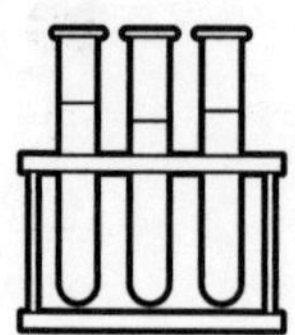

Science Conundrums

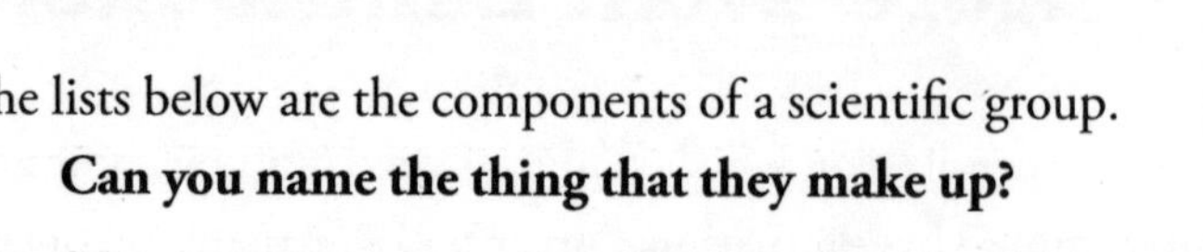

The lists below are the components of a scientific group.
Can you name the thing that they make up?

Movement, Respiration, Sensitivity, Growth, Reproduction, Excretion, Nutrition

Talc, Gypsum, Calcite, Fluorite, Apatite, Orthoclase feldspar, Quartz, Topaz, Corundum, Diamond

Troposphere, Stratosphere, Mesosphere, Thermosphere, Ionosphere, Exosphere, Magnetosphere

Phenylanine, Valine, Threonine, Tryptophan, Isoleucine, Methionine, Histidine, Arginine, Leucine, Lysine

Olfactory, Optic, Oculomotor, Trochlear, Trigeminal, Abducens, Facial, Acoustic, Glassopharyngeal, Vagus, Spinal Accessory, Hypoglossal

Frictional, Tension, Normal, Air Resistance, Applied, Spring, Gravitational, Electrical, Magnetic

Mare Imbrium, Mare Serenitatis, Mare Tranquillitatis, Mare Fecunditatis, Mare Crisium, Mare Nectaris, Mare Nubium, Mare Humorum, Mare Vaporum, Oceanus Procellarum, Mare Frigoris

Stem, meristem, nodes, veins, stomata, axil, bud, pedicel, petal, sepal, filament

Canis Major Dwarf, Segue 1, Sagittarius Dwarf Spheroidal, Ursa Major II Dwarf, Reticulum II Dwarf

Amobarbital, Aprobarbital, Pentobarbital, Thiopental, Alcohol, Chloral hydrate, Chlordiazepoxide, Lorazepam, Triazolam

Answers on page 190

Political Quotes

Here are some quotes about politics: some of these were said by well-known politicians, some by humorists or political commentators. **For how many of them can you identify the original speaker?**

1. *'The oppressed are allowed once every few years to decide which particular representatives of the oppressing class are to represent and repress them.'*

2. *'If you live long enough, you'll make mistakes. But if you learn from them, you'll be a better person. It's how you handle adversity, not how it affects you. The main thing is never quit, never quit, never quit.'*

3. *'Ask not what your country can do for you; ask what you can do for your country.'*

4. *'There comes a time when one must take a position that is neither safe, nor politic, nor popular, but he must take it because conscience tells him it is right.'*

5. *'What difference does it make to the dead, the orphans and the homeless, whether the mad destruction is wrought under the name of totalitarianism or in the holy name of liberty or democracy?'*

6. *'No fresh European war is capable of putting something better in the place of unsatisfactory conditions which exist to-day... The outbreak of such madness without end would lead to the collapse of existing social order in Europe.'*

7. *'They misunderestimated me.'*

8. *'Patriotism is, fundamentally, a conviction that a particular country is the best in the world because you were born in it...'*

9. *'I sincerely believe that banking establishments are more dangerous than standing armies, and that the principle of spending money to be paid by posterity, under the name of funding, is but swindling futurity on a large scale.'*

10. *'Freedom in capitalist society always remains about the same as it was in ancient Greek republics: Freedom for slave owners.'*

11. *'In politics, stupidity is not a handicap.'*

12. *'A change is brought about because ordinary people do extraordinary things.'*

13. *'It has been said that Democracy is the worst form of government except all those other forms that have been tried from time to time.'*

14. *'Speeches made to the people are essential to the arousing of enthusiasm for a war.'*

15. *'Anyone who is capable of getting themselves made President should on no account be allowed to do the job.'*

Answers on page 190

The Names of Plants

Here is a list of the botanical names of plants and flowers. **For how many of them can you give the common name?**

Agapanthus

Eryngium

Hippeastrum

Brugmansia

Gypsophila

Campanula

Thunbergia alata

Impatiens

Dianthus

Aquilegia

Centaurea

Narcissus

Dicentra cucullaria

Oenothera

Tanacetum parthenium

Leucadendron

Anthurium

Myosotis

Mirabilis jalapa

Digitalis

Phalaris arundinacea

Delphinium consolida

Syringa

Calendula

Aster

Paeonia

Antirrhinum

Matthiola

Helianthus

Lathyrus

Dianthus barbatus

Gladiolus

Gerbera

Anemone

Achillia

Answers on page 190

Fields of Knowledge

This is a list of descriptions of areas of scientific, artistic, or philosophical knowledge.

Can you give the correct name for each description?

1. **The study of timekeeping**
2. **The art of curing and stuffing animals**
3. **The art of printing or using type**
4. **The science of movement and dynamics in a flow of air or gas**
5. **The science of sound**
6. **The study of ancient plants**
7. **The study of ants**
8. **The study of birds**
9. **The study of coats of arms**
10. **The study of coins**
11. **The study of diseases; epidemics**
12. **The study of earthquakes**
13. **The study of excrement or obscene literature**
14. **The study of forces that produce or change motion**

Answers on page 191

15. The study of funguses

16. The study of material human remains

17. The study of language

18. The study of the mechanics of gases

19. The study of movement in liquids

20. The study of poisons

21. The study of postage stamps

22. The study of shells

23. The study of skin

24. The study of the surface of the earth and its inhabitants

25. The study of the structure of the body

26. The study of tumours

27. The study of weather

28. The art of bell-ringing

29. The study of the underpinning of morality

30. The study of volcanoes and volcanic activity

Animal Babies

Can you remember the name (or names) for the young of these species?

Aardvark
Alpaca, llama, guanaco or vicuña
Ant
Anteater
Ape
Bat
Beaver
Boar
Cod
Coyote
Dove or pigeon
Duck
Eagle
Eel
Falcon or hawk
Fox
Frog/toad
Goat
Goose
Guineafowl
Hare
Hedgehog
Hippopotamus
Horse
Jellyfish

Kangaroo
Monkey
Mosquito
Mouse
Newt
Opossum
Otter
Owl
Oyster
Platypus
Porcupine
Puffin
Rabbit
Raccoon
Rhinoceros
Salmon or trout
Seal
Sheep
Skunk
Snake
Spider
Swan
Turkey
Walrus
Wolf

Answers on page 192

Capitals of Europe

Can you name the capitals of the following European countries?

Albania
Austria
Belarus
Belgium
Bosnia-Herzegovina
Bulgaria
Cyprus
Czech Republic
Denmark
Estonia
Finland
France
Germany
Greece
Hungary
Ireland
Italy
Kosovo

Latvia
Lithuania
Luxembourg
Malta
Montenegro
Netherlands
Norway
Poland
Portugal
Romania
Serbia
Slovakia
Slovenia
Spain
Switzerland
Sweden
United Kingdom

Answers on page 193

Standard units

Can you name the standard units for:

1. Distance
2. Mass
3. Time
4. Electric charge
5. Temperature
6. Mole
7. Candela

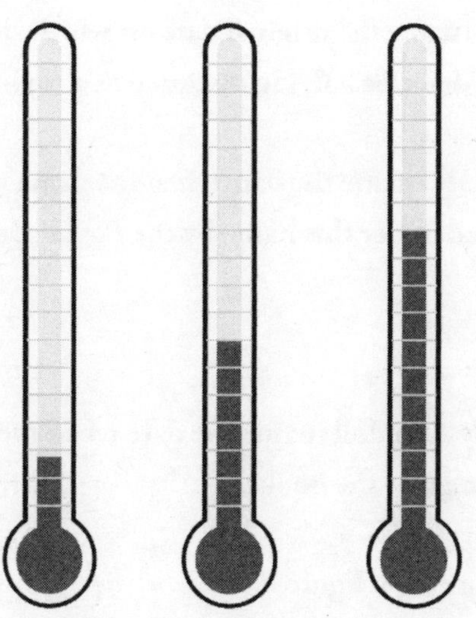

Answers on page 193

Toys and Games that Became Crazes

Can you name the original release date of the following toys?

1. Twister

2. Silly Putty
3. Scrabble

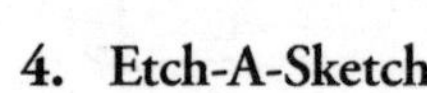

4. Etch-A-Sketch
5. Mr. Potato Head
6. Frisbee (name the original date on which this term was used to describe a flying disc used as a toy)
7. Monopoly (name the date when the game was first marketed under this name by the Parker Brothers)
8. Barbie doll
9. Raggedy Ann doll (name the date when the doll was first sold alongside the books)
10. G. I. Joe action figure
11. Hungry Hungry Hippos

12. Cabbage Patch Kids doll (name the date when they went into mass production)

13. Beanie Babies
(the date when the toys were first available)

14. Tickle Me Elmo

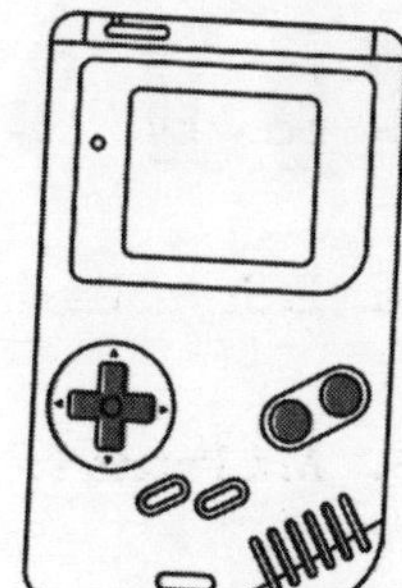

15. Tamagotchis

16. Bratz Dolls

17. Sylvanian Families

18. GameBoy (name the date it was first released in Japan by Nintendo)

19. Power Rangers figures. The launch of *Power Rangers* on TV led to huge sales of the figurines over subsequent years. But when was the TV launch?

20. Furby

21. Trivial Pursuit

22. Toy Story Buzz Lightyear toy

23. Teksta the Robotic Puppy

Answers on page 194

Dinosaur Silhouettes

How many of these dinosaur profiles can you name?

5

6

7

8

9

Answers on page 194

Shakespeare Characters

Lots of people can name Shakespeare plays, but you are more likely to know the characters' names if you have actually seen or read the actual play. So how well do you know the Bard?

Here's a list of characters, name the play they appear in.

Portia

Falstaff (name all three plays he appears in)

Mercutio

The Three Witches

Horatio

Tybalt

Bianca Minola

Goneril

Nick Bottom

Lavinia

Petruchio

King Claudius

Mustardseed

Duke Orsino

Lady Macduff

Tullus Aufidius

Caliban

Katerina

Polonius

Adriana

Hippolyta

Aaron the Moor

Alciabades

Brabantio

Solinus, the Duke of Ephesus

Margarelon

Thomas Cranmer

Autolycus

Berowne

Duncan

Owen Glendower

Kate Keepdown

The Duke of Berry

Bromodideuterio

The Boatswain

Desdemona

The Bear

Answers on page 195

After the Music Died

The early part of the 21st century has been notable for how many of the greats of 20th-century popular music have sadly passed away. Here are just a few of the musical greats we have lost: how much can you remember about their careers?

MICHAEL JACKSON

Can you name Michael Jackson's ten bestselling songs of all time? (including the Jackson Five material)

How many of his ten solo albums can you name? (released during his lifetime)

DAVID BOWIE

The great shapeshifter died in January 2016, just days after the release of his final *Blackstar* album. **Can you name his ten most downloaded songs ever?** (not including collaborations)

Can you name all Bowie's 1970s albums in the correct order?

WHITNEY HOUSTON

The great singer's career spanned a variety of styles and brought her huge success before her sad death in 2012. **Can you name her ten bestselling hits?** (as measured by the Billboard charts)

LOU REED

Lou Reed was possibly New York's finest musician-poet. **How many of his 22 studio albums can you name?**

PRINCE

Prince, who was often described as the Mozart of funk, died in 2016. **Can you name his ten bestselling hits? Can you also name Prince's first ten studio albums?**

AMY WINEHOUSE

Amy Winehouse had only achieved a small part of her extraordinary potential when she died in 2012 at the age of 27 (joining the list of musicians like Kurt Cobain, Brian Jones and Janis Joplin in the club of performers who died at that age). **How many of the songs on her two studio albums 'Frank' and 'Back to Black' can you name (ignoring hidden tracks)?**

GEORGE MICHAEL

George Michael was another singer-songwriter of genius, who died in 2016. **Can you name his ten bestselling songs ever?** (Wham! songs are included). **How many of George's five solo albums can you name?**

Answers on page 195

Martin Scorsese

How many of the great director's feature films can you name? Ignore documentaries and short films. Get double points if you can name his first three movies, as they are less well known…

1.	**14.**
2.	**15.**
3.	**16.**
4.	**17.**
5.	**18.**
6.	**19.**
7.	**20.**
8.	**21.**
9.	**22.**
10.	**23.**
11.	**24.**
12.	**25.**
13.	**26.**

Answers on page 198

The Discovery of the Elements

Before 1650, humanity had only discovered and identified 13 of the chemical elements. **Can you name those 13?**

Can you name the discoverers of the following elements and put them in order of the date of their discovery?

Aluminium

Argon

Chromium

Iridium

Nickel

Nitrogen

Palladium

Plutonium

Radium

Ruthenium

Technetium

Tennessine

Thulium

Answers on page 199

Geometrical Shapes

Can you give the formal mathematical names for the shapes below?

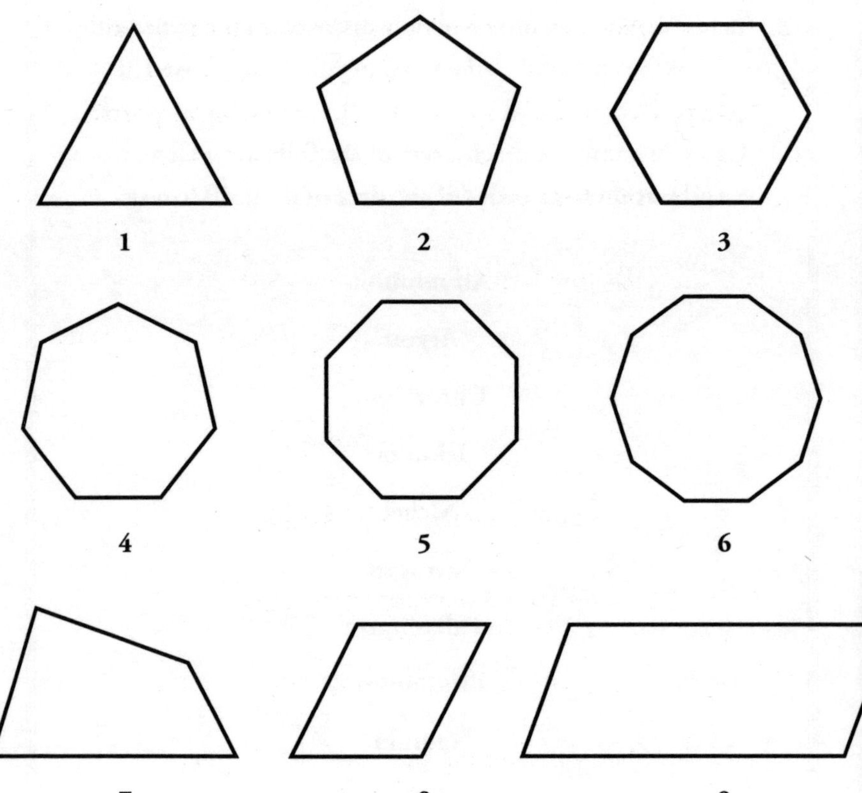

Answers on page 200

IATA Codes

International Airports are identified using unique identifiers, three letters known as an IATA code. (IATA stands for International Air Transport Association, the trade association of the major airlines.)

Do you know the IATA code for the following airports?

Hartsfield-Jackson Atlanta International Airport

Beijing Capital International Airport

Los Angeles International Airport

Tokyo Haneda Airport

Dubai International Airport

O'Hare International Airport

London Heathrow Airport

Shanghai Pudong International Airport

Hong Kong International Airport

Paris-Charles de Gaulle Airport

Dallas/Fort Worth International Airport

Guangzhou Baiyun International Airport

Seoul Incheon International Airport – Incheon

Answers on page 200

Amsterdam Airport Schiphol

Frankfurt Airport

Singapore Changi Airport

Suvarnabhumi Airport

Denver International Airport

Indira Gandhi International Airport – Delhi

Soekarno–Hatta International Airport

John F. Kennedy International Airport

Kuala Lumpur International Airport

Madrid Barajas Airport

San Francisco International Airport

Chengdu Shuangliu International Airport

Shenzhen Bao'an International Airport

Orlando International Airport

McCarran International Airport

Barcelona–El Prat Airport

Toronto Pearson International Airport

The World's Tallest Mammals

Can you name the world's eight tallest land mammals?

1.
2.
3.
4.
5.
6.
7.
8.

How about the world's six smallest land mammals?

1.
2.
3.
4.
5.
6.

Answers on page 200

Cartoons

Can you identify these animated movies from the brief descriptions of the plots?

1. A young girl who has recently moved to San Francisco struggles with her emotions.
2. Fleeing from an evil queen, a young girl takes refuge with some miners.
3. A young boy and an old man travel to Paradise Falls using balloons.
4. A father searches the oceans for his missing son.
5. A chieftain's daughter sets sail in search of a wind god.
6. A lying puppet has to prove his worth.
7. The new toy in a house comes into conflict with the de facto leader of the crew.
8. A one-eyed boy teams up with Monkey and Beetle and sets off on a quest.
9. A young Viking has to capture dragons.
10. A sheep tries to con his owner, but after an unfortunate mishap with a caravan has to rectify his mistakes.
11. A Japanese boy goes in search of his missing dog.
12. An elephant gets drunk and finds himself stuck up a tree.

13. **A waste-collecting robot meets a much more technologically advanced female robot.**

14. **A rat and a garbage boy team up in a restaurant-based caper.**

15. **A 27-year-old Japanese girl reminisces about life in Tokyo while on a journey.**

16. **A superhero comes out of retirement, along with his family.**

17. **The captain of a submarine sets off to free a distant land from some blue villains.**

18. **The Pumpkin King decides to celebrate Christmas for a change.**

19. **Monsters who get their power from human screams meet a little girl.**

20. **A boy befriends a huge alien robot.**

Answers on page 201

Famous Roads and Streets

Can you identify the following streets and roads from the information provided?

1. Fictional home to Sherlock Holmes.
2. Famously revisited in a classic Bob Dylan album.
3. Many believe this is the road that Jesus carried his cross down to his crucifixion.
4. New York's original Skid Row, once home to CBGBs
5. A London street full of doctors.
6. One of the oldest, busiest markets to be found in Old Delhi.
7. The street in Dublin that links St Stephen's Square with Trinity College.
8. The centre of Swinging London in the 1960s.
9. A pedestrian tourist magnet in Barcelona.
10. The home of theatre in New York.

11. The street that links tre Arc de Triomphe and the Place de la Concorde.

12. The street that links Edinburgh Castle and Holyrood Palace.

13. Home to the famous stars commemorating great actors and actresses.

14. Location of the studio in which the Beatles recorded their eleventh studio album.

15. The most famous street dedicated to gambling in the world.

16. Home of the New York Stock Exchange.

Answers on page 201

British Prime Ministers

Can you name all the 20th- century prime ministers of the United Kingdom?

Note that several names should appear more than once on the list, so one point for each spell those prime ministers were in office for.

Answers on page 202

French Presidents

Can you name all 10 post-1947 presidents of France?

1.

2.

3.

4.

5.

6.

7.

8.

9.

10.

Answers on page 203

Twenty Books by Famous Scientists

Here are some classic titles about science: most are by well-known scientists, while a few are classic books about science.
Can you name the authors?

1. *The Origin of Species*
2. *Radioactive Substances*
3. *The Double Helix*
4. *The Realm of the Nebulae*
5. *Silent Spring*
6. *Pale Blue Dot: A Vision of the Human Future in Space*
7. *Survival of the Wisest*
8. *Surely You're Joking, Mr. Feynman!*
9. *The Sky Is Not the Limit: Adventures of an Urban Astrophysicist*
10. *A Brief History of Time*
11. *The Mirage of a Space between Nature and Nurture*
12. *The Selfish Gene*
13. *The Discovery of the Tomb of Tutankhamen*
14. *Coming of Age in Samoa*
15. *The Periodic Table*
16. *Disclosing the Past: An Autobiography*
17. *Shadows of the Mind: A Search for the Missing Science of Consciousness*
18. *How the Universe Got Its Spots: Diary of a Finite Time in a Finite Space*
19. *Dialogue Concerning the Two Chief World Systems*
20. *What is Life?*

Answers on page 203

Suit Patterns

Can you identify the patterns of these types of cloth, commonly used to manufacture men's suits in particular?

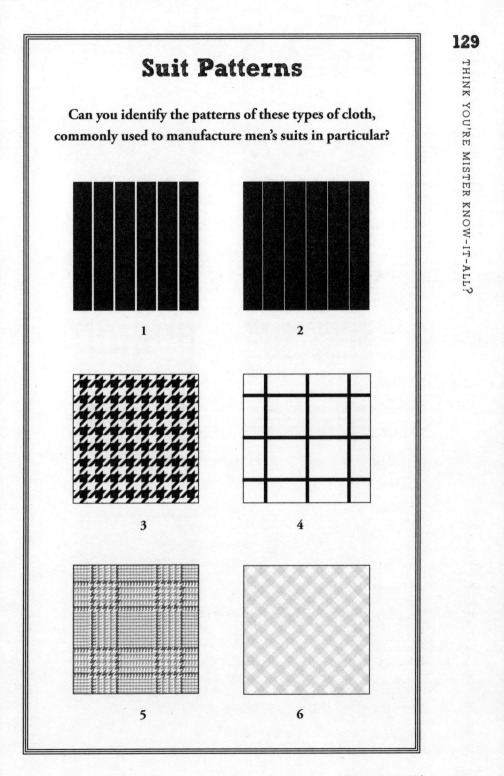

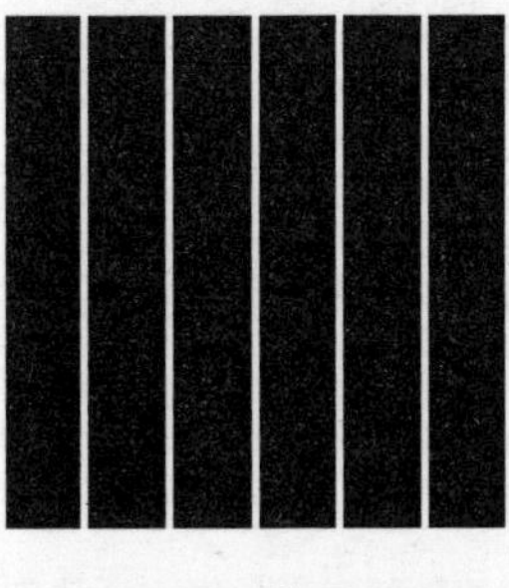

1

2

3

4

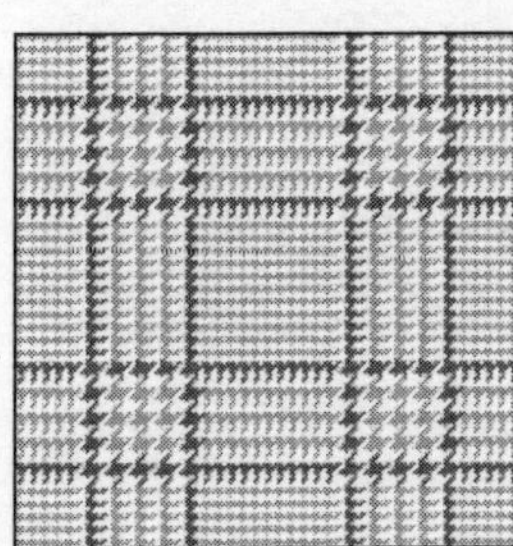

5

6

Answers on page 204

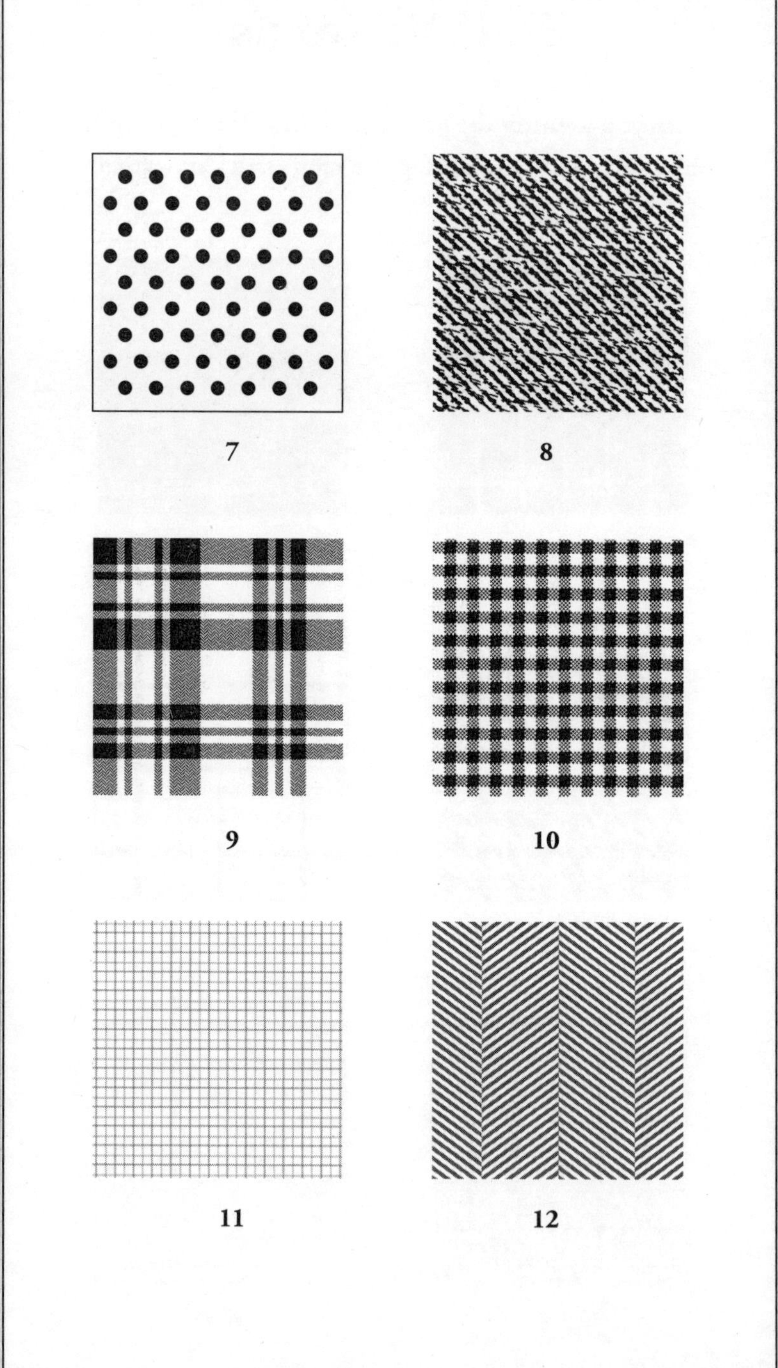
7
8
9
10
11
12

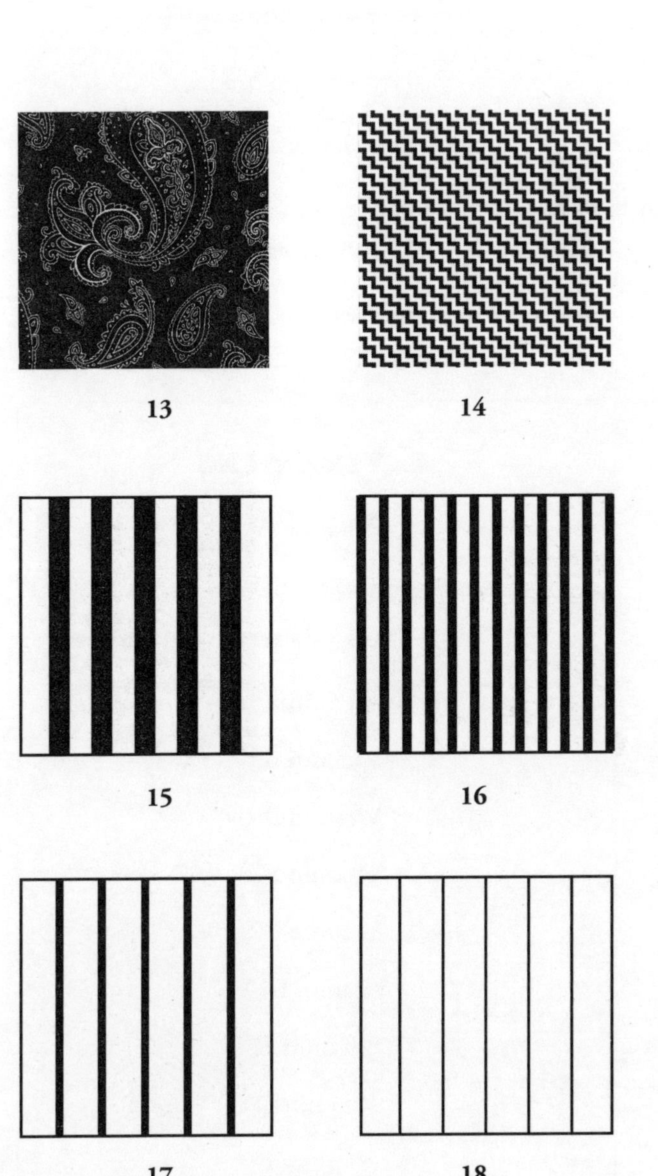
13
14
15
16
17
18

Know Your Vitamins

Here are two lists.

List A is the name of a vitamin.

List B is a selection of food items that can provide that vitamin in a balanced diet. The lists are each in a different order.

Can you match up the items in each list correctly?

A: VITAMINS

Vitamin A

Vitamin B1

Vitamin B2

Vitamin B3

Vitamin B5

Vitamin B6

Vitamin B7

Vitamin B9

Vitamin B12

Vitamin C

Vitamin D

Vitamin E

Vitamin K

B: FOOD SOURCES

Dairy products, bananas, green beans, asparagus

Eggs, liver, sardines, shiitake

Fish, liver and dairy products, ripe yellow fruits, leafy vegetables, carrots, pumpkin, squash, spinach

Fruits and vegetables, liver

Fruits and vegetables, nuts and seeds, and seed oils

Leafy green vegetables, including spinach, egg yolks

Leafy vegetables, bread, pasta, cereal, liver

Meat, avocados, broccoli

Meat, fish, eggs, many vegetables, mushrooms, tree nuts

Meat, poultry, eggs, milk, fish

Meat, vegetables, nuts, bananas

Pork, oatmeal, brown rice, vegetables, potatoes, liver, eggs

Raw egg yolk, peanuts, liver, green vegetables

Answers on page 206

The Novels of Anne Tyler

How many of the 23 novels of the brilliant Baltimore novelist can you name?

1.	**13.**
2.	**14.**
3.	**15.**
4.	**16.**
5.	**17.**
6.	**18.**
7.	**19.**
8.	**20.**
9.	**21.**
10.	**22.**
11.	**23.**
12.	

Answers on page 207

Tools for Every Purpose

How handy are you about the house and garden: do you think you would recognize or be able to use any kind of tool there is out there? **Well, can you identify the purpose of each of these strange-sounding tools and/or who would use it?**

Ball-peen Hammer

Manual Impact Driver

Miter Saw

Dogleg Reamer

Stork Beak Pliers

Tooth Chisel

Triple Tap

Cape Chisel

Stubby Nail Eater

Duplex Rabbet Plane

Egg Beater Drill

Flat Bastard File

Spud Wrench

Shingle Froe

Halligan Bar

Pneumatic Planishing Hammer

Ryoba Saw

Inflatable Shim

Torpedo Level

Darby

Gorilla Gripper

Ice Pet

Big Gus

Answers on page 207

Diseases

Below are the Latin or other names for some major or widespread diseases: the name given is either the name of the disease, or of the pathogen that causes it.

Can you identify the diseases?

Bacillus anthracis

Clostridium botulinum

Bartonella henselae

Varicella zoster virus (VZV)

Vibrio cholerae

Acute viral rhinopharyngitis

Corynebacterium diphtheriae

Neisseria gonorrhoeae

Legionella pneumophila

Mycobacterium leprae and Mycobacterium lepromatosis

Plasmodium species

Rubeola

Rubulavirus

Sarcoptes scabiei

Clostridium tetani

Answers on page 209

The Movies of Stanley Kubrick

Can you name the 13 feature films directed by Stanley Kubrick in his remarkable cinematic career?
And can you give the correct original release date?

Kubrick also directed three documentary shorts?
Can you name them?

In addition, there was one final film for which he was the producer based on an original story outline that he provided.
Can you name it?

1.	**10.**
2.	**11.**
3.	**12.**
4.	**13.**
5.	**14.**
6.	**15.**
7.	**16.**
8.	**17.**
9.	

Answers on page 210

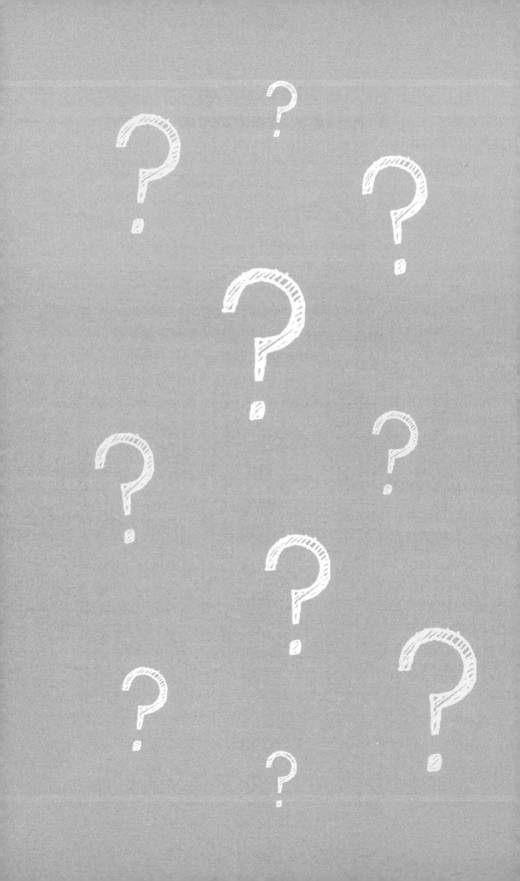

ANSWERS

THE SOLAR SYSTEM AND ITS MOONS

1. Jupiter
(diameter = 142,800 km)
2. Saturn
(diameter = 120,660 km)
3. Uranus
(diameter = 51,118 km)
4. Neptune
(diameter = 49,528 km)
5. Earth
(diameter = 12,756 km)
6. Venus
(diameter = 12,104 km)
7. Mars
(diameter = 6,787 km)
8. Mercury
(diameter = 4,879.4 km)

Moons:
Mars: Phobos
Jupiter: Ganymede
Saturn: Titan
Uranus: Titania
Neptune: Triton
Pluto: Charon

AFRICAN NATIONS

Algeria
Angola
Benin
Botswana
Burkina Faso
Burundi
Cabo Verde (or Cape Verde)
Cameroon
Central African Republic
Chad
Comoros
Congo
Côte d'Ivoire (or The Ivory Coast)
Djibouti
DR Congo
Egypt
Equatorial Guinea
Eritrea
Eswatini (formerly Swaziland)
Ethiopia
Gabon
Gambia
Ghana
Guinea
Guinea-Bissau
Kenya

Lesotho
Liberia
Libya
Madagascar
Malawi
Mali
Mauritania
Mauritius
Morocco
Mozambique
Namibia
Niger
Nigeria
Rwanda
São Tomé & Principe
Senegal
Sierra Leone
Somalia
South Africa
South Sudan
Sudan
Tanzania
The Seychelles
Togo
Tunisia
Uganda
Zambia
Zimbabwe

THE FOUR ELEMENTS

Aries, Taurus, Gemini, Cancer, Leo, Virgo, Libra, Scorpio, Sagittarius, Capricorn, Aquarius, Pisces

Fire Signs:
Aries, Leo, Sagittarius

Earth Signs:
Taurus, Virgo, Capricorn

Air Signs:
Gemini, Libra, Aquarius

Water Signs:
Cancer, Scorpio, Pisces

CHINESE YEARS

Rat (Water)
Ox (Earth)
Tiger (Wood)
Rabbit (Wood)
Dragon (Earth)
Snake (Fire)
Horse (Fire)
Goat/Sheep (Earth)
Monkey (Metal)
Rooster (Metal)
Dog (Earth)
Pig (Water)

TURNING POINTS IN WORLD HISTORY

1. 3rd Century BC
2. 50 CE
3. 570
4. 800
5. 1066
6. 1095–1099
7. *c.* 1150
8. 1215
9. 1227
10. 1453
11. 1455
12. 1492
13. 1504
14. 1519
15. 1522
16. 1543
17. 1619
18. 1642
19. 1687
20. 1773
21. 1776
22. 1807
23. 1812
24. 1848
25. 1859
26. 1860
27. 1867
28. 1869
29. 1876
30. 1903
31. 1905
32. 1906
33. 1919
34. 1922
35. 1929
36. 1933
37. 1944
38. 1947
39. 1949
40. 1963
41. 1963
42. 1969
43. 1989
44. 1994
45. 2001

TWENTY CARTOON CHARACTERS

Mickey Mouse 1928
Donald Duck 1934
Yogi Bear 1958 (as a supporting character on *The Huckleberry Hound Show*)
The Flintstones 1960
Popeye (in print) 1929

Felix the Cat 1919
Betty Boop 1930
Scooby-Doo 1969
Roger Rabbit 1988
The Simpsons (as a separate show) 1989
Beavis and Butthead 1993
The cast of South Park 1997
Hong Kong Phooey 1974
Tom and Jerry 1940
Shrek 2001
Ren and Stimpy 1991
Wile E. Coyote and Road Runner 1949
Foghorn Leghorn 1946
Daffy Duck 1937
Pluto 1930

THE MOVIE APPEARANCES OF MARILYN MONROE

1. *Dangerous Years* (1947)
2. *Scudda Hoo! Scudda Hay!* (1948)
3. *Ladies of the Chorus* (1948)
4. *Love Happy* (1949)
5. *A Ticket to Tomahawk* (1950)
6. *The Asphalt Jungle* (1950)
7. *All About Eve* (1950)
8. *The Fireball* (1950)
9. *Right Cross* (1951)
10. *Home Town Story* (1951)
11. *As Young as You Feel* (1951)
12. *Love Nest* (1951)
13. *Let's Make It Legal* (1951)
14. *Clash by Night* (1952)
15. *We're Not Married!* (1952)
16. *Don't Bother to Knock* (1952)
17. *Monkey Business* (1952)
18. *O. Henry's Full House* (1952)
19. *Niagara* (1953)
20. *Gentlemen Prefer Blondes* (1953)
21. *How to Marry a Millionaire* (1953)
22. *River of No Return* (1954)
23. *There's No Business Like Show Business* (1954)
24. *The Seven Year Itch* (1955)
25. *Bus Stop* (1956)
26. *The Prince and the Showgirl* (1957)
27. *Some Like It Hot* (1959)

28. *Let's Make Love* (1960)
29. *The Misfits* (1961)
30. *Something's Got to Give* (1962–)

COMPUTER KEYBOARD

QWERTYUIOP
ASDFGHJKL
ZXCVBNM

FUN WITH ALPHABETS

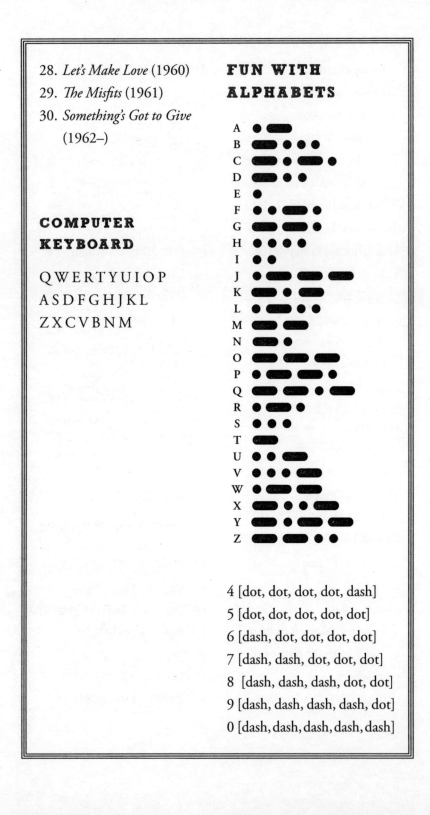

4 [dot, dot, dot, dot, dash]
5 [dot, dot, dot, dot, dot]
6 [dash, dot, dot, dot, dot]
7 [dash, dash, dot, dot, dot]
8 [dash, dash, dash, dot, dot]
9 [dash, dash, dash, dash, dot]
0 [dash,dash,dash,dash,dash]

The Russian Alphabet: 33
The Greek Alphabet: 24
The Spanish Alphabet: 27
The Japanese Alphabet (in the hiragana or katakana syllabic scripts rather than Kanji): 46, or 71 including diacritics
The Turkish Alphabet: 29

DISNEY ANIMALS

Archimedes
The Captain and Sergeant Tibbs
Al
Shere Khan
Roquefort
Orville
Tod and Copper
Mufasa, Sarabi, Scar
Mushu
Tant and Terkor
Marlin
Buck
Tiana and Naveen (who are both frogs for part of the movie)
Sven

QUICKIES

The Burj Khalifa
Mount Everest
Ojos del Salado
The Nile
The Mariana Trench
The Trans-Siberian Railway
Hartsfield–Jackson Atlanta
Lake Baikal
The Pan-American Highway
the Antarctic Polar Desert, the Arctic Polar Desert, the Sahara Desert (well done if you got the first two…)
The Makhonjwa Mountains or Barberton Greenstone Belt in South Africa and Eswatini/Swaziland.

GREAT FIRST LINES

Goodfellas, Henry Hill (Ray Liotta)
Fear & Loathing In Las Vegas, Raoul Duke (Johnny Depp)
Reservoir Dogs, Mr Brown (Quentin Tarantino)

Rebecca, Mrs de Winter (Joan Fontaine)

Million Dollar Baby, Scrap (Morgan Freeman)

Black Swan, Nina Sayers (Natalie Portman)

Terminator 2: Judgment Day, Sarah Connor (Linda Hamilton)

Trainspotting, Renton (Ewan McGregor)

The Lord Of The Rings: The Fellowship Of The Ring, Galadriel (Cate Blanchett)

Field Of Dreams, Ray Kinsella (Kevin Costner)

Raging Bull, Jake La Motta (Robert De Niro)

Ferris Bueller's Day Off, Ferris Bueller (Matthew Broderick)

The Rules of Attraction, Lauren (Shannyn Sossoman)

Spider-Man, Peter Parker (Tobey Maguire)

CULTURAL SYMBOLS

1. Ankh
2. Gordian Knot
3. Flower of Life
4. Jerusalem Cross
5. Menorah
6. Tajitu or Yin-Yang Symbol
7. Eye of Horus
8. Maltese Cross
9. Vesica Pisces
10. Ouroboros
11. Pentacle
12. Chi-Rho
13. Maneki-Neko (or Beckoning Cat)
14. Hammer and Sickle
15. Star and Crescent
16. Shrivatsa or Infinite Knot

THE OLD RED, WHITE AND BLUE

Australia
Cambodia
Chile
Republic of China (Taiwan and surrounding islands)
Cuba
Czech Republic
Faroe Islands (Danish autonomous country)
France
Iceland
North Korea
Laos
Liberia
Luxembourg
Nepal
Netherlands
New Zealand
Norway
Panama
Russia
Slovakia
Thailand
United Kingdom
United States of America

LINGUA FRANCA

1. Mandarin Chinese (1.1 billion speakers)
2. English (983 million speakers)
3. Hindustani (544 million speakers: the collective name for Hindi and Urdu, which are dialects of the same language)
4. Spanish (527 million speakers)
5. Arabic (422 million speakers)
6. Malay (281 million speakers)
7. Russian (267 million speakers)
8. Bengali (261 million speakers)
9. Portuguese (229 million speakers)
10. French (229 million speakers)
11.
12. Native Americans in Nebraska
13. South Africa
14. North east India

15. China
16. Nigeria
17. Philippines
18. Cambodia
19. Bangladesh
20. Cornwall in England
21. Brittany in France

Hungarian
Polish
Swahili
Turkish
French
Irish
Zulu
Malay
Norwegian
Hawaiian

THE GOLFING GREATS

Jack Nicklaus	18
Tiger Woods	15
Walter Hagen	11
Ben Hogan	9
Gary Player	9
Tom Watson	8
Bobby Jones	7
Arnold Palmer	7
Gene Sarazen	7
Sam Snead	7
Harry Vardon	7
Nick Faldo	6
Lee Trevino	6
Seve Ballesteros	5
James Braid	5
Phil Mickelson	5
Byron Nelson	5
J.H. Taylor	5
Peter Thomson	5

TWENTY JAMES BOND CHARACTERS

1. *A View to a Kill*
2. *Casino Royale*
3. *Skyfall*
4. *From Russia With Love*
5. *The Spy Who Loved Me*
6. *Thunderball*
7. *Octopussy*
8. *Licence to Kill*
9. *Live and Let Die*
10. *Moonraker*
11. *GoldenEye*
12. *Die Another Day*
13. *GoldenEye*
14. *From Russia with Love*
15. *Diamonds Are Forever*
16. *Quantum of Solace*
17. *Goldfinger*
18. *Dr. No*
19. *You Only Live Twice*
20. *The Man with the Golden Gun*

CLASSICAL CONUNDRUMS

The Olympians
The Seven Wonders of the Ancient World
The Charities (or Graces)
The Titans
The Flavian Dynasty
The Six Simple Machines
The Four Great Inventions (of China)
The Four Classic Novels (China)

GREAT ARTWORKS

1. Johannes Vermeer
2. Sandro Botticelli
3. Vincent van Gogh
4. James McNeill Whistler
5. Gustav Klimt
6. Jan van Eyck
7. Hieronymus Bosch
8. Frida Kahlo
9. Hokusai
10. Georges Seurat
11. Pablo Picasso
12. Pieter Bruegel the Elder
13. Édouard Manet
14. Piet Mondrian
15. Francisco Goya
16. Caspar David Friedrich
17. Yayoi Kusama
18. Bridget Riley
19. Théodore Géricault
20. Edward Hopper
21. Marcel Duchamp

WORLD'S GREAT TOURIST ATTRACTIONS

1. Prague, Czech Republic
2. Istanbul, Turkey
3. Granada, Spain
4. Paris, France
5. St. Petersburg, Russia
6. Paris, France
7. San Francisco, USA
8. Rio de Janeiro, Brazil
9. San Francisco, USA
10. The Vatican, Vatican City
11. Northern Territory, Australia (closed to the public in 2019)
12. Barcelona, Spain
13. Abu Dhabi, United Arab Emirates
14. Agra, India
15. Andes Mountains, Peru
16. Siem Reap, Cambodia
17. Kuala Lumpur, Malaysia
18. Yucatan, Mexico
19. Bangkok, Thailand
20. New York City, USA
21. Dubai, United Arab Emirates
22. Washington, DC, USA

MULTIPLE OSCARS

Katharine Hepburn
Morning Glory (1933)
Guess Who's Coming to Dinner (1967)
The Lion in Winter (1968)
On Golden Pond (1981)

Daniel Day-Lewis
My Left Foot (1989)
There Will Be Blood (2007)
Lincoln (2012)

Meryl Streep
Sophie's Choice (1982)
The Iron Lady (2011)
Kramer vs. Kramer (1979)

Jack Nicholson
One Flew Over the Cuckoo's Nest (1975)
Terms of Endearment (1983)
As Good as It Gets (1997)

Ingrid Bergman
Gaslight (1944)
Anastasia (1956)
Murder on the Orient Express (1974)

Walter Brennan
Come and Get It (1936)
Kentucky (1938)
The Westerner (1940)

OSCARS: BEST INTERNATIONAL FEATURE FILM

1. *Bicycle Thieves*, Italy
2. *Rashomon*, Japan
3. *La Strada*, Italy
4. *My Uncle*, France
5. *The Virgin Spring*, Sweden
6. *Closely Watched Trains*, Czechoslovakia
7. *The Discreet Charm of the Bourgeoisie*, France
8. *The Tin Drum*, Germany
9. *Babette's Feast*, France
10. *Cinema Paradiso*, Italy
11. *Belle Epoque*, Spain
12. *Burnt by the Sun*, Russia
13. *Life is Beautiful*, Italy
14. *All About My Mother*, Spain
15. *Crouching Tiger, Hidden Dragon*, Taiwan
16. *The Lives of Others*, Germany

17. *A Separation*, Iran
18. *Roma*, Mexico

HISTORY OF TEXTILES

The cotton plant (the boll that grows around the seeds)
The cocoons of the mulberry silkworm
The fur of angora rabbits (mixed with sheep's wool)
The hair of the Indian Cashmere goat
Pineapples
Plant pulp
Glass fibres coated with Teflon

Sericulture (silkmaking)
Edmund Cartwright
Eli Whitney
James Hargreaves
Barthélemy Thimonnier (a French tailor) in 1830

1. Herringbone
2. Arrowhead
3. Cross-stitch
4. Open chain
5. Chain
6. Blanket

FICTIONAL DETECTIVES

M.C. Beaton
Michael Dibdin
Jussi Adler-Olsen
Earl Derr Biggers
Keigo Higashino
Jo Nesbo
Andrea Camilleri
Colin Dexter
Ian Rankin
Kate Atkinson
Sue Grafton
Henning Mankell
Stieg Larsson
Manuel Vázquez Montalbán
Raymond Chandler
Nicolas Freeling
Alexander McCall Smith
Janet Evanovich
Kathy Reichs
Sara Paretsky

THE SEQUEL

1. *Chronicles of Riddick*
2. *Magnum Force*
3. *Funeral in Berlin*
4. *Be Cool*
5. *S.Darko*
6. *The Dark Knight*
7. *Dumb and Dumberer*
8. *Alvin and the Chipmunks: The Squeakquel*
9. *Fierce Creatures*
10. *Life During Wartime*
11. *The Color of Money*
12. *The Two Jakes*
13. *The Evening Star*
14. *The Black Bird*
15. *Staying Alive*
16. *Sanjuro*
17. *Herbie Rides Again*
18. *Shock Treatment*
19. *Desperado*
20. *For A Few Dollars More**

* Lose a point if you fell for the nudge towards *The Good, the Bad and the Ugly* in the preamble to that quiz.

MAMMOTH ANIMALS

1. Goliath beetle
2. Chinese salamander
3. Ostrich
4. Saltwater crocodile
5. Whale shark
6. Brown bear or polar bear
7. Giraffe
8. African elephant

ASIAN CAPITALS

1. Kabul
2. Baku
3. Dhaka
4. Thimpu
5. Beijing (formerly Peking)
6. Nai Dilli (or New Delhi)
7. Tehran
8. Baghdad
9. Tokyo
10. Vientiane (Viangchan, Vieng Chan)
11. Kuala Lumpur
12. Ulaanbaatar (Ulan Bator)
13. Islamabad
14. Manila

15. Riyadh
16. Seoul
17. Colombo
18. Damascus
19. Dushanbe
20. Bangkok
21. Lhasa
22. Ankara
23. Abu Dhabi
24. Tashkent
25. Hanoi

FAMOUS PHILOSOPHICAL QUOTES

Socrates
Ludwig Wittgenstein
René Descartes
Friedrich Nietzsche
John Stuart Mill
Voltaire
Ludwig Wittgenstein
Aristotle
John Locke
Søren Kierkegaard
Friedrich Nietzsche
Karl Marx
Aristotle
Baruch Spinoza
Jean-Paul Sartre
Socrates
Jean-Jacques Rousseau
Aristotle
John Stuart Mill
Jean-Paul Sartre

DOG BREEDS

1. Afgan hound
2. Border collie
3. Corgi
4. Dachshund
5. English bulldog
6. French bulldog
7. German shepherd
8. Siberian husky
9. Irish setter
10. Jack Russell terrier
11. King Charles spaniel
12. Labrador retriever
13. Pit bull
14. Rough collie
15. Giant schnauzer
16. Viszla
17. Wolfhound
18. Chihuahua
19. Pug
20. St Bernard

TWENTY QUESTIONS: THE BIRTH OF SOCIAL MEDIA

1. 1980
2. 1997
3. 1999
4. 1999
5. 2003
6. 2003
7. 2004
8. 2005
9. 2006
10. 2006
11. 2010
12. 2010
13. 2011
14. 2011
15. 2012
16. 2012
17. 2012
18. 2016
19. 2016
20. 2018

WORLD CUP GLORY

1958

Nils Liedholm

Vavá (2)

Pelé (2)

Zagallo

Agne Simonsson

1962

Josef Masopust

Amarildo Tavares da Silveira

Zito

Vavá

1966

Helmut Haller

Geoff Hurst (3)

Martin Peters

Wolfgang Weber

1970

Pelé

Roberto Boninsegna

Gérson

Jairzinho

Carlos Alberto

1974

Johan Neeskens

Paul Breitner

Gerd Müller

1978

Mario Kempes (2)

Dirk Nanninga

Daniel Bertoni

1982

Paolo Rossi

Marco Tardelli

Alessandro Altobelli

Paul Breitner

1986

José Luis Brown

Jorge Valdano

Karl-Heinz Rummenigge

Rudi Völler

Jorge Burruchaga

1990

Andreas Brehme

1994

No goal scorer

1998

Zinedine Zidane (2)

Emmanuel Petit

2002

Ronaldo (2)

2006

Zinedine Zidane

Marco Materazzi

2010

Andrés Iniesta

2014

Mario Götze

2018

Mario Mandžukić (own goal)

Ivan Perišić

Antoine Griezmann

Paul Pogba

Kylian Mbappe

Mario Mandžukić

STATES OF THE UNION

1. Washington
2. Idaho
3. Montana
4. North Dakota
5. Minnesota
6. Wisconsin
7. Michigan
8. New York
9. Vermont
10. New Hampshire
11. Maine
12. Massachusetts
13. Rhode Island
14. Connecticut
15. New Jersey
16. Delaware
17. Maryland
18. Pennsylvania
19. Virginia
20. North Carolina
21. South Carolina
22. Georgia
23. Florida
24. Alabama
25. Mississipi
26. Louisiana
27. Texas

28. New Mexico
29. Arizona
30. California
31. Oregon
32. Nevada
33. Utah
34. Wyoming
35. Colorado
36. South Dakota
37. Nebraska
38. Iowa
39. Illinois
40. Indiana
41. Ohio
42. West Virginia
43. Kentucky
44. Tennessee
45. Arkansas
46. Oklahoma
47. Kansas
48. Missouri

Missing States:
Hawaii, Alaska

State Capitals
Alabama: Montgomery
Alaska: Juneau
Arizona: Phoenix
Arkansas: Little Rock
California: Sacramento
Colorado: Denver
Connecticut: Hartford
Delaware: Dover
Florida: Tallahassee
Georgia: Atlanta
Hawaii: Honolulu
Idaho: Boise
Illinois: Springfield
Indiana: Indianapolis
Iowa: Des Moines
Kansas: Topeka
Kentucky: Frankfort
Louisiana: Baton Rouge
Maine: Augusta
Maryland: Annapolis
Massachusetts: Boston
Michigan: Lansing
Minnesota: St Paul
Mississippi: Jackson
Missouri: Jefferson City
Montana: Helena
Nebraska: Lincoln
Nevada: Carson City
New Hampshire: Concord

New Jersey: Trenton
New Mexico: Santa Fe
New York: Albany
North Carolina: Raleigh
North Dakota: Bismarck
Ohio: Columbus
Oklahoma: Oklahoma City
Oregon: Salem
Pennsylvania: Harrisburg
Rhode Island: Providence
South Carolina: Columbia
South Dakota: Pierre
Tennessee: Nashville
Texas: Austin
Utah: Salt Lake City
Vermont: Montpelier
Virginia: Richmond
Washington: Olympia
West Virginia: Charleston
Wisconsin: Madison
Wyoming: Cheyenne

TWENTY QUESTIONS: MUSICAL MOMENTS

1. The main difference is that a concerto is in three parts whereas a symphony is made up of four or more parts. In addition, a concerto is usually for a soloist.
2. FAST-SLOW-FAST
3. The word 'philharmonic' translates to 'music lover'. The first use of 'philharmonic' was in London, where an organization was founded in 1813 called the Philharmonic Society.
4. Seven
5. Two violins, one viola, one cello
6. One sung without musical accompaniment
7. Slow, stately
8. Rapid
9. Very loud
10. A type of lullaby
11. Two chords that complete a piece of music
12. Getting quieter
13. A repeated musical phrase or rhythm
14. A piece written for eight voices or instruments
15. Minim

16. Quaver
17. Semi-quaver
18. Crochet
19. Double quaver
20. Demibreve

PLATONIC SOLIDS

1. Tetrahedron
2. Cube
3. Octahedron
4. Dodecahedron
5. Icosahedron

PRIME NUMBERS

2, 3, 5, 7, 11, 13, 17, 19, 23, 29, 31, 37, 41, 43, 47, 53, 59, 61, 67, 71, 73, 79, 83, 89, 97.

CAPITAL CITIES OF SOUTH AMERICA

1. Paraguay
2. Colombia
3. Brazil
4. Argentina
5. Venezuela
6. Guyana
7. Peru
8. Uruguay
9. Ecuador
10. Chile

STRANGE CURRENCIES

Afghani, Afghanistan
Argentine Peso, Argentina
Australian Dollar, Australia
Barbadian Dollar, Barbados
Bulgarian Lev, Bulgaria
Bolivian Boliviano, Bolivia
Brazilian Real, Brazil
Canadian Dollar, Canada
Swiss Franc, Switzerland
Chinese Yuan, China
Colombian Peso, Colombia
Danish Krone, Denmark
Egyptian Pound, Egypt
Georgian Lari, Georgia
Croatian Peso, Croatia
Haitian Gourde, Haiti
Hungarian Forint, Hungary
Israeli Dinar, Israel
Indian Rupee, India
Iraqi Dinar, Iraq

Japanese Yen, Japan
Kenyan Shilling, Kenya
South Korean Won, South Korea
Lebanese Pound, Lebanon
Mexican Peso, Mexico
Malaysian Ringgit, Malaysia
Norwegian Krone, Norway
New Zealand Dollar, New Zealand
Pakistani Rupee, Pakistan
Polish Zloty, Poland
Serbian Dinar, Serbia
Russian Rouble, Russia
Saudi Riyal, Saudi Arabia
Turkish Lira, Turkey
Vietnamese Dong, Vietnam
South African Rand, South Africa

K-POP BANDS

1. BTS
2. Stray Kids
3. EXO
4. Monsta X
5. NCT 127
6. SEVENTEEN
7. BLACKPINK
8. GOT7
9. ATEEZ
10. NCT Dream

EUROPOP HITS

1993
1994
1978
1991
1974
1990
1992
1993
1997
1991
1999

SUMMER OLYMPIC SPORTS

Croquet
Cricket
Jeu de Paume
Lacrosse
Motor boating
Pelota
Polo
Roque racket
Tug of War

NAME THE AUTHOR

1. Haruki Murakami
2. Roberto Bolaño
3. Toni Morrison
4. Margaret Atwood
5. Michel Houellebecq
6. Gunter Grass
7. Aravind Adiga
8. Gabriel García Márquez
9. Ralph Ellison
10. Khaled Hosseini
11. Amy Tan
12. Peter Carey
13. Chinua Achebe
14. William Styron
15. William Faulkner
16. George Orwell
17. Yan Lianke
18. Doris Lessing
19. Mikhail Bulgakov

Nobel Prize Winners:

2000 Gao Xingjian
2001 V. S. Naipaul
2002 Imre Kertész
2003 J. M. Coetzee
2004 Elfriede Jelinek
2005 Harold Pinter
2006 Orhan Pamuk
2007 Doris Lessing
2008 J. M. G. Le Clézio
2009 Herta Müller
2010 Mario Vargas Llosq
2011 Tomas Tranströmer
2012 Mo Yan
2013 Alice Munro
2014 Patrick Modiano
2015 Svetlana Alexievich
2016 Bob Dylan
2017 Kazuo Ishiguro

WHAT'S IN A NAME?

Swaziland
Zaire
Burma
Upper Volta
Kampuchea
Dahomey
The Hashemite Kingdom of Jordan
Persia
Macedonia
Southwest Africa
Gold Coast
French Sudan
Siam

Dutch East Indies
East Pakistan
Ellis Islands
Kingdom of Hejaz and Nejd
New Spain
New Hebrides
British Honduras
Basutoland
Irish Free State
British Mandate of Mesopotamia
Gilbert Islands
Nyasaland

COLOUR

1. Yellow, red, blue
2. Purple, green, orange
3. Red, blue, green
4. Cyan, magenta, yellow, black
5. Pantone's "Colour of the Year" since 2000
6. Red, yellow, violet, purple, brown, yellow, blue, red, yellow
7. Blue, Red, Green, Blue, Green

MIXING UP THE ELEMENTS

1. Sodium, chlorine
2. Copper, tin
3. Nitrogen, hydrogen
4. Silicon, oxygen
5. Calcium, carbon, oxygen
6. Nitrogen, oxygen
7. Sodium, hydrogen, carbon, oxygen
8. Iron, carbon (sometimes alloyed with other metals)

The First Ten Elements:

1. Hydrogen (H)
2. Helium (He)
3. Lithium (Li)
4. Beryllium (Be)
5. Boron (B)
6. Carbon (C)
7. Nitrogen (N)
8. Oxygen (O)
9. Fluorine (F)
10. Neon (Ne)

Label the atom

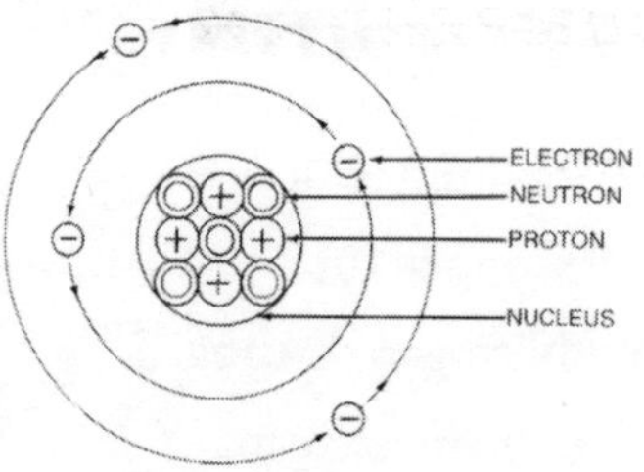

FEMALE INVENTORS AND DISCOVERERS

1. Miracle Mop
2. The computer program (this is arguable, but she was clearly ahead of her time in her elucidation of the concept)
3. The first version of Monopoly (also known as The Landlord's Game)
4. Discovered the elements polonium and radium
5. The coffee filter
6. The bra
7. The chocolate chip cookie
8. COBOL, the first computer language compiler
9. The Nuclear Shell Model
10. Structure of insulin
11. Barbie doll
12. Discoverer of DNA structure
13. Kevlar
14. Discovered that chimpanzees eat meat, and make and use tools
15. Co-inventor of Scotchgard

THE MOVIES OF RICHARD CURTIS

The Tall Guy, 1989
Four Weddings and a Funeral, 1994
Bean, 1997
Notting Hill, 1999
Bridget Jones's Diary, 2001
Love Actually, 2003
Bridget Jones: The Edge of Reason, 2004
The Boat That Rocked, 2009
War Horse, 2011
About Time, 2013
Trash, 2014
Mamma Mia! Here We Go Again, 2018
Yesterday, 2019

THE WIZARD OF OZ TRIVIA

1. Judy Garland
2. Frank Morgan
3. Ray Bolger
4. Jack Haley
5. Bert Lahr
6. Billie Burke
7. Margaret Hamilton
8. Clara Blandick
9. Terry the dog
10. Buddy Ebsen
11. Silver
12. L. Frank Baum

THE GAMES COMPENDIUM

Chess

Pawn
Knight
King
Queen
Bishop
Rook

Poker hands

Royal flush
Straight flush
Four of a kind
Full house
Flush
Straight
Three of a kind
Two pairs
Pair
High card

Backgammon

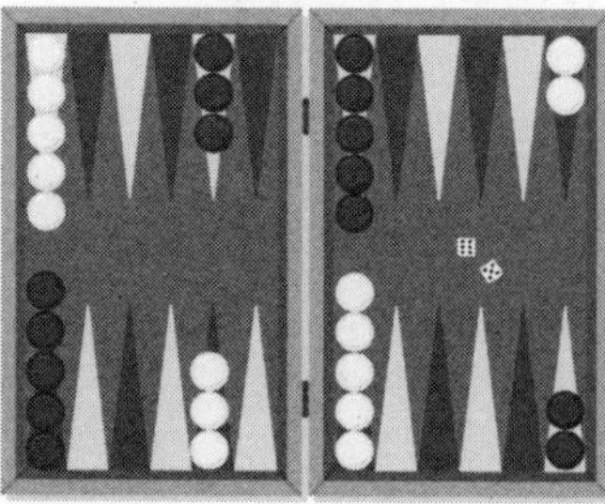

Snooker

Red

Yellow

Green

Brown

Blue

Pink

Black

(The white ball is the one that the snooker player can directly hit: if it is pocketed they are penalized.)

ALL THE SEVENS

1. Prudence, Justice, Temperance, Courage, Faith, Hope, Charity
2. Grumpy, Happy, Sleepy, Bashful, Sneezy, Dopey, Doc
3. Yul Brynner, Eli Wallach, Steve McQueen, Charles Bronson, Robert Vaughn, Brad Dexter, James Coburn, Horst Buchholz
4. Pride, Greed, Lust, Envy, Gluttony, Wrath, Sloth
5. The Arctic Ocean, the North Atlantic Ocean, the South Atlantic Ocean, the Indian Ocean, the North Pacific Ocean, the South Pacific Ocean, the Southern (or Antarctic) Ocean
6. Red, orange, yellow, green, blue, indigo, violet
7. Aventine, Caelian, Capitoline, Esquiline, Palatine, Quirinal, Viminal
8. Gold, silver, copper, tin, lead, iron, mercury

WHICH CONTINENT?

Tallest Mountains
Asia: Mount Everest
South America: Aconcagua
North America: Mount McKinley
Africa: Mount Kilimanjaro
Europe: Mount Elbrus
Antarctica: Vinson Massif
Australasia: Mount Kosciusko

Longest Rivers
Africa: Nile River
Asia: Yangtze River
Australia: Murray-Darling River
Europe: Volga River
North America: Mississippi-Missouri River
South America: Amazon River

THE LONG AND SHORT OF IT

1. 1,000
2. 5,280
3. 1,000
4. 16
5. 60
6. 10,000
7. 97
8. 10,080
9. 2,240
10. 100,000
11. 39,370
12. 304.8
13. 10.76
14. 708.74
15. 3.53
16. 1.15
17. 1
18. 28.32
19. 35.25
20. 5.88 trillion

THE CLASSICAL ORCHESTRA

The standard orchestra was: **a string section** consisting of first and second violins, violas, cellos (also known as violincellos), and double basses; **a woodwind section** including two flutes, two oboes, two clarinets, two bassoons; **a brass section** of two or four horns, two trumpets; and **a percussion section** of two timpani.

However, if you have named any of the following instruments, you don't lose a point as they were innovations introduced (mostly by Haydn) gradually through the classical period: clarinets as part of the woodwind section; as additional percussion instruments: the triangle, hand cymbals, and bass drum.

Famous works

1. Edvard Grieg
2. Antonio Vivaldi
3. Richard Wagner
4. Gustav Holst
5. Claude Debussy
6. Johann Sebastian Bach
7. Pyotr Ilyich Tchaikovsky
8. Erik Satie
9. Edward Elgar
10. Georges Bizet
11. Wolfgang Amadeus Mozart
12. Ludwig van Beethoven

MUSICAL MODES

Ionian, Dorian, Phrygian, Lydian, Mixolydian, Aeolian and Locrian

CLASSIC PLAYS

The Ancients

Sophocles
Aristophanes
Menaechmus Plautus

16th and 17th centuries

Christopher Marlowe
William Shakespeare
Ben Jonson
John Webster
Lope de Vega
Pedro Calderón de la Barca
Molière
Jean Racine
Aphra Behn
Thomas Otway

18th and 19th centuries

Carlo Goldoni
Oliver Goldsmith
Richard Brinsley Sheridan
Pierre-Augustin Caron de Beaumarchais
Friedrich Schiller
Heinrich von Kleist
Henrik Ibsen
Leo Tolstoy
August Strindberg
Frank Wedekind
Oscar Wilde
Anton Chekhov

20th and 21st centuries

J. M. Barrie
George Bernard Shaw
James Joyce
Sean O'Casey
Ben Hecht and Charles MacArthur
Sophie Treadwell
Noël Coward
Federico García Lorca
Bertolt Brecht
Eugene O'Neill
Tennessee Williams
Eugène Ionesco
Terence Rattigan
Arthur Miller
Harold Pinter
Alan Ayckbourn
Wole Soyinka
Brian Friel
Edward Albee

DEM BONES

Top of the spine
Base of the thumb: a carpal bone
The heel bones
The foot
Middle ear
The bone that joins the shoulder and elbow
Upper jaw bones
Collarbone
The smaller of the bones that join the elbow to the wrist
Upper toe
Cheekbone
Eye socket
One of the carpal bones in the wrist
Base of the spine (also known as the tailbone)
Inside the nose
Lower back of the skull
Upper leg
In the skull around the ears
The kneecap bones
Finger bones that run from the knuckle to the fingertip

GREAT BATTLES OF THE WORLD

1. The Battle of Marathon
2. The Battle of Gaugamela
3. Battle of the Hydaspes
4. Battle of Changping
5. The Battle of the Metaurus
6. The Battle of the Teutoburg Forest
7. The Battle of Châlons, also called the Battle of the Catalaunian Fields or the Battle of the Catalun.
8. The Battle of Tours, also called the Battle of Poitiers.
9. The Battle of Hastings
10. The Siege of Orléans
11. Defeat of the Spanish Armada
12. The Battle of Blenheim
13. The Battle of Pultowa
14. The Battles of Saratoga
15. The Battle of Valmy
16. The Battle of Waterloo
17. The Battle of Gettysburg

18. The Battle of the Somme
19. The Battle of El Alamein
20. The Battles of Imphal and Kohima

EXPLORING THE UNIVERSE

1. Mercury
2. Mars
3. Saturn (and Huygens landed on Saturn's largest moon Titan)
4. Mars
5. Mercury (following a fly-by of Venus)
6. Venus
7. Mars
8. Ceres (the largest object in the asteroid belt between Mars and Venus)
9. Jupiter
10. Venus
11. Mars
12. Pluto via Jupiter
13. Uranus and Neptune (via Jupiter and Saturn)
14. Halley's Comet
15. The moon
16. Venus
17. Mars (the first robotic Mars rover)
18. Venus
19. Mars
20. First manned moon landing
21. The sun, obviously
22. The first US soft landing on the moon (Luna 9, the Soviet probe, had also made a soft landing earlier in the year, but the name is a bit of a giveaway)
23. Lissajous orbit around the Lagrangian point L2 between the Earth and the sun

HIT SONGS

15 million sellers

1. 'White Christmas'
2. 'Candle in the Wind 1997' / 'Something About the Way You Look Tonight'
3. 'In the Summertime'
4. 'Silent Night'
5. 'Rock Around the Clock'
6. 'I Will Always Love You'
7. 'It's Now or Never'
8. 'We Are the World'
9. 'If I Didn't Care'
10. 'Yes Sir, I Can Boogie'
11. 'My Heart Will Go On'
12. 'All I Want for Christmas Is You'
13. '(Everything I Do) I Do It for You'
14. 'You're the One That I Want'
15. 'Wind of Change'

10 million sellers

1. Gloria Gaynor
2. Prince Nico Mbarga
3. Kyu Sakamoto
4. Trio
5. Gene Autry
6. The Beatles
7. Andrea Bocelli and Sarah Brightman
8. Village People
9. Band Aid
10. Cher
11. Carl Douglas
12. George McCrae
13. Mills Brothers
14. Roger Whittaker
15. ABBA
16. Roy Acuff
17. Paul Anka
18. Toni Braxton
19. George Harrison
20. Los del Río
21. Middle of the Road
22. The Monkees
23. Panjabi MC
24. Patti Page
25. The Penguins
26. Elvis Presley
27. Procol Harum
28. Britney Spears

SPACE FIRSTS

Sputnik, the world's first artificial satellite, launched by the Soviet Union

Laika the dog, who spent seven days in space

Yuri Gagarin

Alan Shepard

John Glenn

Valentina Tereshkova spent three days alone on *Vostok 6*

Cosmonaut Alexei Leonov

Cosmonaut Vladimir Komarov when *Soyuz 2* crashed upon re-entry

Neil Armstrong

Apollo 13

Pioneer 10

Skylab

Viking 1

The space shuttle *Columbia*

Bruce McCandless and Robert Stewart

Christa McAuliffe, when the space shuttle *Challenger* exploded

The Hubble space telescope.

Dennis Tito

Russian cosmonaut Yuri Malenchenko

Cassini-Huygens

THE TENNIS GREATS

Five men's titles or more:

Roger Federer	20
Rafael Nadal	19
Novak Djokovic	16
Pete Sampras	14
Björn Borg	11
Jimmy Connors	8
Ivan Lendl	8
Andre Agassi	8
John McEnroe	7
Mats Wilander	7
Stefan Edberg	6
Boris Becker	6
Rod Laver	5
John Newcombe	5

Three or more men's grand slams in a calendar year:

Mats Wilander

Roger Federer

Jimmy Connors

Rod Laver

Novak Djokovic

Rafael Nadal

Four or more men's grand slams in a calendar year:

Don Budge (1938)

Rod Laver (1962 and 1969)

Five women's titles or more:

Serena Williams	23
Steffi Graf	22
Chris Evert	18
Martina Navratilova	18
Margaret Court	11
Monica Seles	9
Billie Jean King	8
Evonne Goolagong	7
Justine Henin	7
Venus Williams	7
Martina Hingis	5
Maria Sharapova	5

Three or more women's grand slams in a calendar year:

Serena Williams

Billie Jean King

Steffi Graf

Monica Seles

Martina Hingis

Margaret Court

Four or more women's grand slams in a calendar year:

Maureen Connolly (1953)

Margaret Court (1970)

Steffi Graf (1988)

INTERNATIONAL CO-OPERATION

1. The International Olympic Committee
2. The European Union
3. Food and Agriculture Organization (of the UN)
4. World Bank
5. International Committee of the Red Cross
6. North American Free Trade Association
7. NATO
8. Organization for Economic Co-operation and Development
9. United Nations
10. Opec
11. World Trade Organization
12. World Health Organization

WHICH WEDDING ANNIVERSARY?

Ruby: 40th
Iron: 6th
Diamond: 60th
Paper: 1st
Pearl: 30th
Wool/Copper: 7th
Bronze: 8th
Crystal: 15th
Cotton: 2nd
China: 20th
Golden: 50th
Tin/Aluminium: 10th
Leather: 3rd
Linen/Silk: 4th
Wood: 5th
Silver: 25th
Pottery: 9th

TWENTY TRADITIONAL COSTUMES

India, Sri Lanka, Pakistan, Bangladesh and Nepal
Thailand
Panama
Chile
Qatar
Uganda
Iceland
Japan
Indonesia (also worn in Malaysia, Singapore, Brunei, southern Thailand, Cambodia and the Philippines)
Norway
South Korea (known as the Joseon-oth in North Korea)
China (it is also known as the Mao suit)
Germany
Kenya and Tanzania
Scotland
Nepal
Russia
West Africa and parts of North Africa (it is the traditional dress of the Yoruba, a major ethnic group in Nigeria)
Cameroon
Mexico and Central America

RUSSIA'S NEIGHBOURS

China
Norway
Finland
Ukraine
Kazakhstan
Poland
Georgia
Mongolia
Latvia
Estonia
Azerbaijan
Belarus
Lithuania
North Korea

Abkhazia
South Ossettia

Kazakhstan (4,253 miles)

China (13,743 miles)

Canada-USA (5,525 miles)
Argentina-Chile (3,293 miles)

MYTHICAL HYBRIDS

A jackrabbit with antelope horns (North America)
Seal and human (Scottish)
Ant-lion (Christian)
Body of a dog, head and wings of a bird (Persian)
A lion-headed eagle
The head of a bull and the body of a man (Greek)
A donkey-headed camel
A werewolf, so part human, part wolf
A human head and torso and a goat's waist and legs
A chicken-headed dragon or serpent
Head, arms and upper body of a human, the body and legs of a horse (Greek)
Winged horse with dragon scales (China)
A fish with a lion's head (Singaporean)
Half-human, half-hyena (Africa)
Man and monkey (from the mountains of China)
Rabbit with the horn of a unicorn (Arabia)

CLASSICAL MYTHOLOGY

Goddess of Fertility, Love, and Beauty
God of War
Goddess of Wildlife and the Hunt
Goddess of War
Goddess of the Harvest and Fertility
God of the Vine (or Drinking)
God of Wealth
God of Fire
The Messenger
God of the Sea
Goddess of Chance, Fate and Fortune

Jupiter
Juno
Minerva
Neptune
Venus
Mars
Apollo
Diana
Vulcan
Vesta
Mercury
Ceres

GEOLOGICAL TIME PERIODS

Cambrian 570–510 million years ago
Ordovician 510–439 million
Silurian 439–409 million
Devonian 409–363 million
Carboniferous 363–290 million
Permian 290–245 million
Triassic 245–208 million
Jurassic 208–146 million
Cretaceous 146–65 million
Palaeocene 65–56.5 million
Eocene 56.5–35.4 million
Oligocene 35.4–23.3 million
Miocene 23.3–5.2 million
Pliocene 5.2–2.5 million
Pleistocene 2.5 million−12,000 years ago
Holocene 12,000 years ago−present day

DINOSAUR NAMES

1. Roofed Lizard
2. Three Horned Face
3. Tyrant Lizard
4. Quick Thief
5. Deceptive Lizard
6. Double-Beam Lizard
7. Iguana Tooth
8. Arm Lizard
9. Giant Southern Lizard
10. Earth Shaking Lizard
11. Spine Lizard
12. Stiff Lizard
13. Giraffe Titan
14. Lizard From Lesotho
15. The Ridged Lizard

HIGHEST GROSSING MOVIES BY YEAR

21st century

2000 *Mission: Impossible 2*
2001 *Harry Potter and the Philosopher's Stone*
2002 *The Lord of the Rings: The Two Towers*
2003 *The Lord of the Rings: The Return of the King*
2004 *Shrek 2*
2005 *Harry Potter and the Goblet of Fire*
2006 *Pirates of the Caribbean: Dead Man's Chest*
2007 *Pirates of the Caribbean: At World's End*
2008 *The Dark Knight*
2009 *Avatar*
2010 *Toy Story 3*
2011 *Harry Potter and the Deathly Hallows – Part 2*
2012 *The Avengers*
2013 *Frozen*
2014 *Transformers: Age of Extinction*
2015 *Star Wars: The Force Awakens*
2016 *Captain America: Civil War*
2017 *Star Wars: The Last Jedi*
2018 *Avengers: Infinity War*
2019 *Avengers: Endgame*

Last 50 years of 20th century

1950 *Cinderella*
King Solomon's Mines
1951 *Quo Vadis*
1952 *This Is Cinerama*
The Greatest Show on Earth
1953 *Peter Pan*
The Robe
1954 *Rear Window*
White Christmas
20,000 Leagues Under the Sea
1955 *Lady and the Tramp*
Cinerama Holiday
Mister Roberts
1956 *The Ten Commandments*
1957 *The Bridge on the River Kwai*

1958 *South Pacific*
1959 *Ben-Hur*
1960 *Swiss Family Robinson*
Spartacus
Psycho
1961 *One Hundred and One Dalmatians*
West Side Story
1962 *Lawrence of Arabia*
How the West Was Won
The Longest Day
1963 *Cleopatra*
From Russia with Love
1964 *My Fair Lady*
Goldfinger
Mary Poppins
1965 *The Sound of Music*
1966 *The Bible: In the beginning*
Hawaii
Who's Afraid of Virginia Woolf?
1967 *The Jungle Book*
The Graduate
1968 *2001: A Space Odyssey*
Funny Girl
1969 *Butch Cassidy and the Sundance Kid*
1970 *Love Story*
Airport
1971 *The French Connection*
Fiddler on the Roof
Diamonds Are Forever
1972 *The Godfather*
1973 *The Exorcist*
The Sting
1974 *The Towering Inferno*
Blazing Saddles
1975 *Jaws*
1976 *Rocky*
1977 *Star Wars*
1978 *Grease*
1979 *Moonraker*
Rocky II
1980 *The Empire Strikes Back*
1981 *Raiders of the Lost Ark*
1982 *E.T. the Extra-Terrestrial*
1983 *Return of the Jedi*
1984 *Indiana Jones and the Temple of Doom*
1985 *Back to the Future*
1986 *Top Gun*
1987 *Fatal Attraction*
1988 *Rain Man*
1989 *Indiana Jones and the Last Crusade*

1990 *Ghost*
1991 *Terminator 2: Judgment Day*
1992 *Aladdin*
1993 *Jurassic Park*
1994 *The Lion King*
1995 *Toy Story*
Die Hard with a Vengeance
1996 *Independence Day*
1997 *Titanic*
1998 *Armageddon*
1999 *Star Wars: Episode I – The Phantom Menace*

All-time highest grossing movies adjusted for inflation:

1. *Gone with the Wind* (1939)
2. *Avatar* (2009)
3. *Titanic* (1997)
4. *Star Wars* (1977)
5. *Avengers: Endgame* (2019)
6. *The Sound of Music* (1965)
7. *E.T. the Extra-Terrestrial* (1982)
8. *The Ten Commandments* (1956)
9. *Doctor Zhivago* (1965)
10. *Star Wars: The Force Awakens* (2015)

A CORNUCOPIA OF VILLAINY

1. *The Strange Case of Dr. Jekyll and Mr. Hyde*, Robert Louis Stevenson
2. '*The Final Problem*', Sir Arthur Conan Doyle
3. *Rebecca*, Daphne du Maurier
4. *David Copperfield*, Charles Dickens
5. *East of Eden*, John Steinbeck
6. *Wuthering Heights*, Emily Brontë
7. *Frankenstein*, Mary Shelley
8. *Red Dragon*, Thomas Harris
9. *Never Mind*, Edward St. Aubyn
10. *The Girl With The Dragon Tattoo*, Stieg Larsson
11. *The Talented Mr. Ripley*, Patricia Highsmith
12. *One Flew Over The Cuckoo's Nest*, Ken Kesey
13. *Uncle Tom's Cabin*, Harriet Beacher Stowe
14. *Psycho*, Robert Bloch
15. *1984*, George Orwell
16. *101 Dalmatians*, Dodie Smith
17. *American Psycho*, Bret Easton Ellis
18. *Lolita*, Vladimir Nabokov
19. *The Lord of the Rings*, J.R.R.Tolkien
20. *Misery*, Stephen King
21. *Catch-22*, Joseph Heller
22. *Othello*, William Shakespeare
23. *Tess of the D'Urbervilles*, Thomas Hardy
24. *Crime and Punishment*, Fyodor Dostoevsky

TWENTY QUESTIONS: BIOLOGY

Taxonomic ranks
Genus
Family
Order
Class
Phylum
Kingdom
Domain

Main branches of biology
Botany
Zoology
Microbiology

Six kingdoms of life
Archaebacteria
Eubacteria
Protista (or Protozoa)
Fungi
Plantae (Plants)
Animalia (Animals)

Four main elements
Carbon
Hydrogen
Oxygen
Nitrogen

THE MOVIES OF DANIEL DAY-LEWIS

Gandhi, 1982
The Bounty, 1984
My Beautiful Laundrette, 1985
A Room with a View, 1985
Nanou, 1986
The Unbearable Lightness of Being, 1988
Stars and Bars, 1988
My Left Foot, 1989
Eversmile, New Jersey, 1989
The Last of the Mohicans, 1992
The Age of Innocence, 1993
In the Name of the Father, 1993
The Crucible, 1996
The Boxer, 1997
Gangs of New York, 2002
The Ballad of Jack and Rose, 2005
There Will Be Blood, 2007
Nine, 2009
Lincoln, 2012
Phantom Thread, 2017

Uncredited role
Sunday Bloody Sunday, 1971

CHINESE DYNASTIES

Xia (Hsia) 2205–1766 BC
Shang 1766–1122 BC
Zhou (Chow) 1122–770 BC
Spring & Autumn Annals 770–476 BC
Warring States 476 – 221 BC
Qin (Chin) 221–206 BC
Han 206 BC–AD 220
Three Kingdoms AD 220–265
Jin (Tsin) AD 265–420
Southern and Northern AD 420–580
Sui AD 589–618
Tang AD 618–907
Five Dynasties AD 907–960
Song (Sung) 960–1280
Yuan 1280–1368
Ming 1368–1644
Qing (Ching) 1644–1911
Republic of China 1911–1949
People's Republic of China 1949–present

NORTH TO SOUTH

City	Degrees North
Reykjavík, Iceland	64
Helsinki, Finland	60
Oslo, Norway	59
Aberdeen, Scotland	57
Moscow, Russia	55
Manchester, England	53
Berlin, Germany	52
Paris, France	48
Zürich, Switzerland	47
Milan, Italy	45
Rome, Italy	41
Beijing, China	39
Lisbon, Portugal	38
Tokyo, Japan	35
Shanghai, China	31
Cairo, Egypt	30
Mecca, Saudi Arabia	21
Mexico City, Mexico	19
Rangoon, Myanmar	16
Manila, Philippines	14
Panama City, Panama	8
Kuala Lumpur, Malaysia	3
Singapore, Singapore	1

City	Degrees South
Kinshasa, Congo	4
Jakarta, Indonesia	6
Darwin, Australia	12
Rio de Janeiro, Brazil	22
Brisbane, Australia	27
Perth, Australia	31
Cape Town, South Africa	33
Sydney, Australia	34
Auckland, New Zealand	36
Wellington, New Zealand	41
Hobart, Tasmania	42

TIME ZONES

Amsterdam, Netherlands: 6:00 p.m.

Athens, Greece: 7:00 p.m.

Bangkok, Thailand: midnight

Beijing, China: 1:00 a.m.

Berlin, Germany: 6:00 p.m.

Birmingham, England: 5:00 p.m.

Buenos Aires, Argentina: 2:00 p.m.

Cairo, Egypt: 7:00 p.m.

Cape Town, South Africa: 7:00 p.m.

Helsinki, Finland: 7:00 p.m.

Jakarta, Indonesia: midnight

Madrid, Spain: 6:00 p.m.

Mecca, Saudi Arabia: 8:00 p.m.

Mexico City, Mexico: 11:00 a.m.

Nairobi, Kenya: 8:00 p.m.

Odessa, Ukraine: 7:00 p.m.

Rio de Janeiro, Brazil: 2:00 p.m.

Rome, Italy: 6:00 p.m.

Shanghai, China: 1:00 a.m.

Stockholm, Sweden: 6:00 p.m.

Tripoli, Libya: 7:00 p.m.
Vladivostok, Russia: 3:00 a.m.
Wellington, New Zealand: 5:00 a.m.

THE ALBUMS OF BOB DYLAN

Bob Dylan, 1962
The Freewheelin' Bob Dylan, 1963
The Times They Are A-Changin', 1964
Another Side of Bob Dylan, 1964
Bringing It All Back Home, 1965
Highway 61 Revisited, 1965
Blonde on Blonde, 1966
John Wesley Harding, 1967
Nashville Skyline, 1969
Self Portrait, 1970
New Morning, 1970
Pat Garrett & Billy the Kid [Soundtrack], 1973
Dylan, 1973
Planet Waves, 1974
Blood on the Tracks, 1975
The Basement Tapes, 1975
Desire, 1976
Street Legal, 1978
Slow Train Coming, 1979
Saved, 1980
Shot of Love, 1981
Infidels, 1983
Empire Burlesque, 1985
Knocked Out Loaded, 1986
Down in the Groove, 1988
Oh Mercy, 1989
Under the Red Sky, 1990
Good as I Been to You, 1992
World Gone Wrong, 1993
Time Out of Mind, 1997
Love and Theft, 2001
Modern Times, 2006
Together Through Life, 2009
Christmas in the Heart, 2009
Tempest, 2012
Shadows in the Night, 2015
Fallen Angels, 2016
Triplicate, 2017

PRESIDENTS OF THE USA

William McKinley (1897–1901)
Theodore Roosevelt (1901–9)
William H. Taft (1909–13)
Woodrow Wilson (1913–21)
Warren Harding (1921–3)
Calvin Coolidge (1923–9)
Herbert Hoover (1929–33)
Franklin D. Roosevelt (1933–45)
Harry S Truman (1945–53)
Dwight Eisenhower (1953–61)
John F. Kennedy (1961–3)
Lyndon B. Johnson (1963–9)
Richard Nixon (1969–74)
Gerald Ford (1974–7)
Jimmy Carter (1977–81)
Ronald Reagan (1981–9)
George H. W. Bush (1989–93)
William J. Clinton (1992–2001)

* You might have missed William McKinley as his presidency started in the 19th century, but he was president until his assassination, six months into his second term. At that point, Theodore Roosevelt was the vice-president, and so he ascended to the presidency.

The first five presidents were:

George Washington (1789–97)
John Adams (1797–1801)
Thomas Jefferson (1801–9)
James Madison (1809–17)
James Monroe (1817–25)

Vice-presidents

Theodore Roosevelt, 1901
Charles Warren Fairbanks, 1905–9
James Sherman, 1909–12
Thomas R. Marshall, 1913–21
Calvin Coolidge, 1921–3
Charles G. Dawes, 1925–9
Charles Curtis, 1929–33
John Nance Garner, 1933–41
Henry A. Wallace , 1941–5
Harry S. Truman, 1945
Alben W. Barkley, 1949–53
Richard M. Nixon, 1953–61
Lyndon B. Johnson, 1961–3
Hubert H. Humphrey, 1965–9
Spiro T. Agnew, 1969–73

Gerald R. Ford, 1973–4
Nelson A. Rockefeller, 1974–7
Walter F. Mondale, 1977–81
George H. W. Bush, 1981–9
Dan Quayle, 1989–93
Albert Gore, 1993–2001

THE MOVIES OF MERYL STREEP

Julia, 1977
The Deer Hunter, 1978
Manhattan, 1979
The Seduction of Joe Tynan, 1979
Kramer vs. Kramer, 1979
The French Lieutenant's Woman, 1981
Still of the Night, 1982
Sophie's Choice, 1982
Silkwood, 1983
Falling in Love, 1984
Plenty, 1985
Out of Africa, 1985
Heartburn, 1986
Ironweed, 1987
A Cry in the Dark, 1988
She-Devil, 1989
Postcards from the Edge, 1990
Defending Your Life, 1991
Death Becomes Her, 1992
The House of the Spirits, 1993
The River Wild, 1994
The Bridges of Madison County, 1995
Before and After, 1996
Marvin's Room, 1996
Dancing at Lughnasa, 1998
One True Thing, 1998
Music of the Heart, 1999
A.I. Artificial Intelligence, 2001
Adaptation, 2002
The Hours, 2002
Stuck on You, 2003
The Manchurian Candidate, 2004
Lemony Snicket's A Series of Unfortunate Events, 2004
Prime, 2005
A Prairie Home Companion, 2006
The Music of Regret, 2006
The Devil Wears Prada, 2006
The Ant Bully, 2006
Dark Matter, 2007
Evening, 2007
Rendition, 2007
Lions for Lambs, 2007

Mamma Mia!, 2008
Doubt, 2008
Julie & Julia, 2009
Fantastic Mr. Fox, 2009
It's Complicated, 2009
The Iron Lady, 2011
Hope Springs, 2012
A Fierce Green Fire, 2013
Out of Print, 2013
August: Osage County, 2013
The Giver, 2014
The Homesman, 2014
Into the Woods, 2014
Ricki and the Flash, 2015
Suffragette, 2015
Florence Foster Jenkins, 2016
We Rise, 2017
The Guardian Brothers, 2017
The Post, 2017
Mamma Mia! Here We Go Again, 2018
Mary Poppins Returns, 2018
The Laundromat, 2019
Little Women, 2019

The uncredited cameo was in *Stuck On You* by the Farrelly Brothers, in which she makes a brief appearance as herself.

MORE THAN LANDLOCKED

Andorra is landlocked by France and Spain
Bhutan is landlocked by India and China
Eswatini is landlocked by South Africa and Mozambique
Liechtenstein is landlocked by Switzerland and Austria
Moldova is landlocked by Ukraine and Romania
Mongolia is landlocked by Russia and China
Nepal is landlocked by India and China

Enclaves:
Lesotho is landlocked by South Africa
San Marino is landlocked by Italy
Vatican City is landlocked by Italy

Doubly landlocked:
Liechtenstein is landlocked by Switzerland and Austria
Uzbekistan is landlocked by

Afghanistan, Kazakhstan, Kyrgyzstan, Tajikistan, and Turkmenistan

SCIENCE CONUNDRUMS

The Vital Signs of Life

The Mohs Scale for measuring the hardness of rock

Layers of the atmosphere

The essential amino acids required by the human body

Nerves of the eye

Types of force

Lunar seas

Parts of the structure of a plant

Galaxies: an extra mark if you knew that these are the five closest galaxies to the Milky Way

Names of sedatives

POLITICAL QUOTES

1. Karl Marx
2. Bill Clinton
3. John F. Kennedy
4. Martin Luther King Jr.
5. Mahatma Gandhi
6. Adolf Hitler
7. George W. Bush
8. George Bernard Shaw
9. Thomas Jefferson
10. Vladimir Lenin
11. Napoleon Bonaparte
12. Barack Obama
13. Winston Churchill
14. Benito Mussolini
15. Douglas Adams

THE NAMES OF PLANTS

African lily

Alpine thistle

Amaryllis

Angel's trumpet

Baby's breath

Bell Flower/Canterbury Bells

Black-eyed Susan

Busy Lizzie

Carnation

Columbine
Cornflower
Daffodil
Dutchman's breeches
Evening primrose
Feverfew
Flame tip
Flamingo flower
Forget-me-not
Four o'clock flower
Foxglove
Gardener's garters
Larkspur
Lilac
Marigold
Michaelmas daisy
Peony
Snapdragon
Stock
Sunflower
Sweet pea
Sweet william
Sword lily
Transvaal daisy
Windflower
Yarrow

FIELDS OF KNOWLEDGE

1. Horology
2. Taxidermy
3. Typography
4. Aerodynamics
5. Acoustics
6. Paleobotany
7. Myrmecology
8. Ornithology
9. Heraldry
10. Numismatics
11. Epidemiology
12. Seismology
13. Scatology
14. Kinetics
15. Mycology
16. Archaeology
17. Linguistics
18. Pneumatics
19. Hydrodynamics
20. Toxicology
21. Philately
22. Conchology
23. Dermatology
24. Geography
25. Anatomy
26. Oncology
27. Meteorology

28. Campanology
29. Ethics
30. Vulcanology

ANIMAL BABIES

Cub or calf

Cria

Antling

Pup

Ape infant

Bat pup

Beaver kitten or kit

Boar shoat, boarlet or piglet

Codling

Pup or whelp

Squab or squeaker

Duckling

Eaglet

Elver

Eyas

Pup, cub or kit

Tadpole/polliwog

Kid

Gosling

Keet

Leveret

Piglet or pup

Calf

Foal, colt (male) or filly (female)

Ephyra

Joey

Infant

Wriggler

Pup or pinky

Eft

Joey

Pup or whelp

Owlet

Spat

Puggle

Porcupette

Puffling

Kitten, kit or bunny

Cub or kit

Calf

Alevin, parr or smolt

Pup

Lamb

Kitten or kit

Snakelet

Spiderling

Cygnet or flapper

Poult, jake (male) or jenny (female)

Cub or pup

Cub, pup or whelp

CAPITALS OF EUROPE

Tirana
Vienna
Minsk
Brussels
Sarajevo
Sofia
Nicosia
Prague
Copenhagen
Tallinn
Helsinki
Paris
Berlin
Athens
Budapest
Dublin
Rome
Prishtina
Riga
Vilnius
Luxembourg
Valletta
Podgorica
Amsterdam
Oslo
Warsaw
Lisbon
Bucharest
Belgrade
Bratislava
Ljubljana
Madrid
Berne
Stockholm
London

STANDARD UNITS

1. Metre
2. Gram (or technically, the kilogram)
3. Second
4. Ampoule
5. Kelvin
6. Atomic mass
7. Luminous intensity

TOYS AND GAMES THAT BECAME CRAZES

1. 1966
2. 1944
3. 1949
4. 1960
5. 1952
6. 1957
7. 1935
8. 1959
9. 1918
10. 1965
11. 1978
12. 1982
13. 1993
14. 1996
15. 1996
16. 2001
17. 1985
18. 1989
19. 1993
20. 1998
21. 1981
22. 1995: this was the year that the movie was released and the toy became a high-demand Xmas toy as the manufacturers had underestimated how successful the movie would be and thus how big demand for the toys would be
23. 2000

DINOSAUR SILHOUETTES

1. Stegosaurus
2. Spinosaurus
3. Velociraptor
4. Brachiosaurus
5. Triceratops
6. Parasaurolophus
7. Tyrannosaurus
8. Pterodactyl
9. Plesiosaurus

SHAKESPEARE CHARACTERS

The Merchant of Venice
Henry IV, Parts I and II, The Merry Wives of Windsor
Romeo and Juliet
Macbeth
Hamlet
Romeo and Juliet
The Taming of the Shrew
King Lear
A Midsummer Night's Dream
Titus Andronicus
Taming of the Shrew
Hamlet
A Midsummer Night's Dream
Twelfth Night
Macbeth
Coriolanus
The Tempest
The Taming of the Shrew
Hamlet
The Comedy of Errors
A Midsummer Night's Dream
Titus Andronicus
Timon of Athens
Othello
The Comedy of Errors
Troilus and Cressida
Henry VIII
The Winter's Tale
Love's Labour's Lost
Macbeth
Henry IV, Part 1
Measure for Measure
Henry V
Cymbeline
The Tempest
Othello
The Winter's Tale

AFTER THE MUSIC DIED

Michael Jackson:
'Billie Jean'
'Earth Song'
'I Want You Back'
'Beat It'
'One Day In Your Life'
'Don't Stop Till You Get Enough'
'Black Or White'
'Man In The Mirror'
'Thriller'
'You Are Not Alone'

Got to Be There
Ben
Music & Me
Forever, Michael

Off the Wall

Thriller

Bad

Dangerous

HIStory: Past, Present and Future, Book I

Invincible

David Bowie:

'Life On Mars'

'Heroes'

'Let's Dance'

'Space Oddity'

'Starman'

'Changes'

'Ashes To Ashes'

'Where Are We Now'

'Rebel Rebel'

'Modern Love'

Hunky Dory

The Rise and Fall of Ziggy Stardust and the Spiders from Mars

Aladdin Sane

Pin Ups

Diamond Dogs

Young Americans

Station to Station

Low

Heroes

Lodger

Whitney Houston

'I Will Always Love You'

'I Wanna Dance With Somebody (Who Loves Me)'

'Greatest Love Of All'

'All The Man That I Need'

'I'm Your Baby Tonight'

'So Emotional'

'How Will I Know"

'Didn't We Almost Have It All'

'Saving All My Love For You'

'Exhale (Shoop Shoop)'

Lou Reed:

Lou Reed

Transformer

Berlin

Sally Can't Dance

Metal Machine Music

Coney Island Baby

Rock and Roll Heart

Street Hassle

The Bells

Growing Up in Public
The Blue Mask
Legendary Hearts
New Sensations
Mistrial
New York
Songs for Drella (with John Cale)
Magic and Loss
Set the Twilight Reeling
Ecstasy
The Raven
Hudson River Wind Meditations
Lulu (with Metallica)

Prince
'When Doves Cry'
'Kiss'
'Let's Go Crazy'
'Cream'
'Batdance'
'Raspberry Beret'
'U Got The Look'
'Purple Rain'
'The Most Beautiful Girl In The World'
'Sign O' The Times'

For You
Prince
Dirty Mind
Controversy
1999
Purple Rain
Around the World in a Day
Parade
Sign o' the Times
Lovesexy

Amy Winehouse
Frank
'Intro/Stronger Than Me'
'You Sent Me Flying/Cherry'
'Know You Now'
'Fuck Me Pumps'
'I Heard Love Is Blind'
'Moody's Mood for Love/ Teo Licks'
'(There Is) No Greater Love'
'In My Bed'
'Take the Box'
'October Song'
'What Is It About Men'
'Help Yourself'

Back to Black
'Rehab'
'You Know I'm No Good'
'Me & Mr Jones'
'Just Friends'

'Back to Black'
'Love Is a Losing Game'
'Tears Dry on Their Own'
'Wake Up Alone'
'Some Unholy War'
'He Can Only Hold Her'
'Addicted'

George Michael
'Faith'
'Careless Whisper'
'One More Try'
'Wake Me Up Before You Go-Go'
'Everything She Wants'
'Father Figure'
'I Knew You Were Waiting (for Me)'
'Monkey'
'I Want Your Sex'
'Praying for Time'

Faith
Listen Without Prejudice Vol. 1
Older
Songs from the Last Century
Patience

MARTIN SCORSESE

1. *Who's That Knocking at My Door*
2. *Bezeten, Het Gat in de Muur*
3. *Boxcar Bertha*
4. *Mean Streets*
5. *Alice Doesn't Live Here Anymore*
6. *Taxi Driver*
7. *New York, New York*
8. *Raging Bull*
9. *The King of Comedy*
10. *After Hours*
11. *The Color of Money*
12. *The Last Temptation of Christ*
13. *Goodfellas*
14. *Cape Fear*
15. *The Age of Innocence*
16. *Casino*
17. *Kundun*
18. *Bringing Out the Dead*
19. *Gangs of New York*
20. *The Aviator*
21. *The Departed*

22. *Shutter Island*
23. *Hugo*
24. *The Wolf of Wall Street*
25. *Silence*
26. *The Irishman*

THE DISCOVERY OF THE ELEMENTS

1. Copper
2. Lead
3. Gold
4. Silver
5. Iron
6. Carbon
7. Tin
8. Sulphur
9. Mercury
10. Zinc
11. Arsenic
12. Antimony
13. Bismuth

Nickel	1751	F. Cronstedt
Nitrogen	1772	D. Rutherford
Chromium	1794	N. Vauquelin
Palladium	1802	W. H. Wollaston
Iridium	1803	S. Tennant
Aluminium	1825	H. C. Ørsted
Ruthenium	1844	K. Claus
Thulium	1879	T. Cleve
Argon	1894	Lord Rayleigh and W. Ramsay
Radium	1898	P. and M. Curie
Technetium	1937	C. Perrier and E. Segrè
Plutonium	1940-1	A team led by G. T. Seaborg
Tennessine	2009	A team led by Y. Oganessian

GEOMETRICAL SHAPES

1. Triangle
2. Pentagon
3. Hexagon
4. Heptagon
5. Octagon
6. Decagon
7. Trapezium
8. Rhombus
9. Parallelogram

IATA CODES

ATL
PEK
LAX
HND
DXB
ORD
LHR
PVG
HKG
CDG
DFW
CAN
ICN
AMS
FRA
SIN
BKK
DEN
DEL
CGK
JFK
KUL
MAD
SFO
CTU
SZX
MCO
LAS
BCN
YYZ

THE WORLD'S TALLEST MAMMALS

Giraffe
Elephant
Ostrich
Bear
Moose
Camel
Horse
Bison

The World's Smallest Mammals

Pygmy possum
American shrew mole
Pygmy jerboa
Etruscan shrew
Bumblebee bat
Mouse lemur

CARTOONS

Inside Out
Snow White and the Seven Dwarfs
Up
Finding Nemo
Moana
Pinocchio
Toy Story
Kubo and the Two Strings
How To Train Your Dragon
Shaun the Sheep Movie
Isle of Dogs
Dumbo
WALL-E
Ratatouille
Only Yesterday
The Incredibles
Yellow Submarine
The Nightmare Before Christmas
Monsters, Inc.
The Iron Giant

FAMOUS ROADS AND STREETS

1. Baker Street, London
2. Highway 61, USA
3. Via Dolorosa, Jerusalem
4. The Bowery, New York City
5. Harley Street, London
6. Chandni Chowk, Delhi
7. Grafton Street, Dublin
8. Carnaby Street, London
9. La Rambla, Barcelona
10. Broadway, New York City
11. Champs-Élysées, Paris
12. The Royal Mile, Edinburgh
13. Hollywood Boulevard, Los Angeles
14. Abbey Road, London
15. The Vegas Strip, Las Vegas
16. Wall Street, New York City

BRITISH PRIME MINISTERS

Tony Blair, 1997-2007
John Major, 1990-1997
Margaret Thatcher, 1979-1990
James Callaghan, 1976-1979
Harold Wilson, 1974-1976
Edward Heath, 1970-1974
Harold Wilson, 1964-1970
Sir Alec Douglas-Home, 1963-1964
Harold Macmillan, 1957-1963
Sir Anthony Eden, 1955-1957
Sir Winston Churchill, 1951-1955
Clement Attlee, 1945-1951
Winston Churchill, 1940-1945
Neville Chamberlain, 1937-1940
Stanley Baldwin, 1935-1937
Ramsay MacDonald, 1929-1935
Stanley Baldwin, 1924-1929
Ramsay MacDonald, 1924
Stanley Baldwin, 1923
Andrew Bonar Law, 1922-1923
David Lloyd George, 1916-1922
H.H. Asquith, 1908-1916
Sir Henry Campbell-Bannerman, 1905-1908
Arthur James Balfour, 1902-1905
Marquess of Salisbury, 1895-1902

FRENCH PRESIDENTS

Vincent Auriol, 1947-1954
René Coty, 1954-1959
Charles de Gaulle, 1959-1967
Georges Pompidou, 1969-1974
Valéry Giscard d'Estaing, 1974-1981
François Mitterrand, 1981-1995
Jacques Chirac, 1995-2007
Nicolas Sarkozy, 2007-2012
François Hollande, 2012-2017
Emmanuel Macron, 2017-present

TWENTY BOOKS BY FAMOUS SCIENTISTS

1. Charles Darwin
2. Marie Curie
3. James Watson
4. Edwin Hubble
5. Rachel Carson
6. Carl Sagan
7. Jonas Salk
8. Richard Feynman
9. Neil deGrasse Tyson
10. Stephen Hawking
11. Evelyn Fox Keller
12. Richard Dawkins
13. Howard Carter
14. Margaret Mead
15. Primo Levi
16. Mary Leakey
17. Rog
18. Primo Levi
19. Galileo Galilei
20. Erwin Schrödinger

SUIT PATTERNS

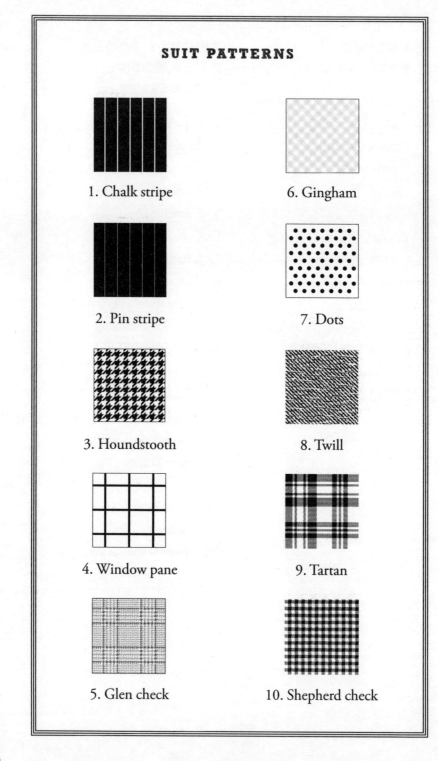

1. Chalk stripe

6. Gingham

2. Pin stripe

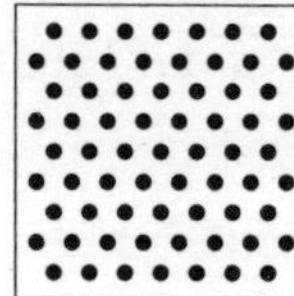

7. Dots

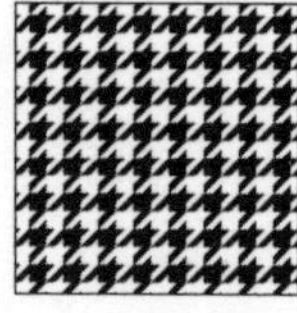

3. Houndstooth

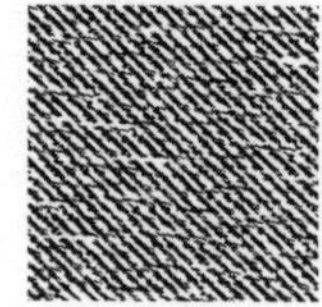

8. Twill

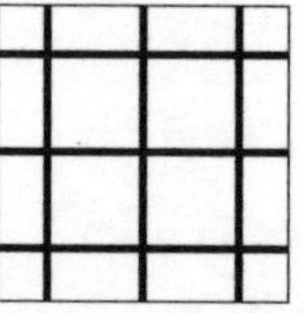

4. Window pane

9. Tartan

5. Glen check

10. Shepherd check

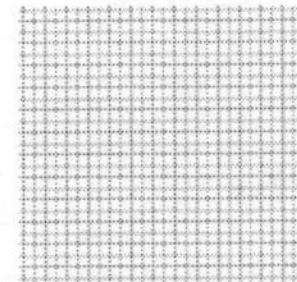

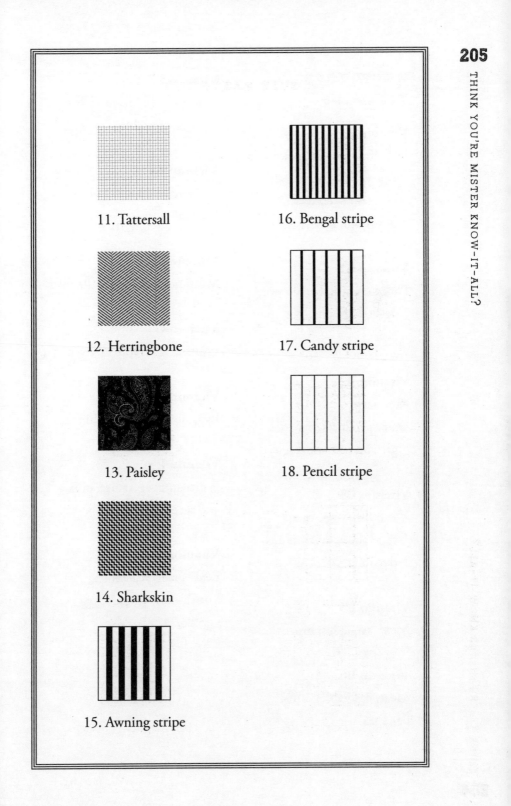

11. Tattersall

12. Herringbone

13. Paisley

14. Sharkskin

15. Awning stripe

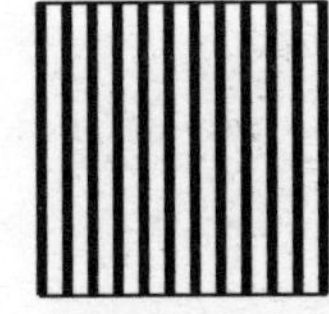

16. Bengal stripe

17. Candy stripe

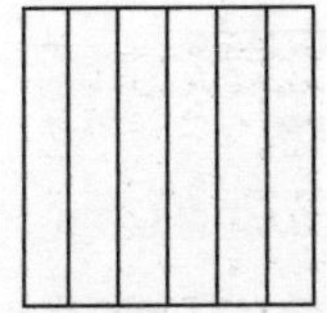

18. Pencil stripe

KNOW YOUR VITAMINS

Vitamin A
Fish, liver and dairy products, ripe yellow fruits, leafy vegetables, carrots, pumpkin, squash, spinach

Vitamin B1
Pork, oatmeal, brown rice, vegetables, potatoes, liver, eggs

Vitamin B2
Riboflavin
Dairy products, bananas, green beans, asparagus

Vitamin B3
Meat, fish, eggs, many vegetables, mushrooms, tree nuts

Vitamin B5
Meat, avocados, broccoli

Vitamin B6
Meat, vegetables, nuts, bananas

Vitamin B7
Raw egg yolk, peanuts, liver, green vegetables

Vitamin B9
Leafy vegetables, bread, pasta, cereal, liver

Vitamin B12
Meat, poultry, eggs, milk, fish

Vitamin C
Fruits and vegetables, liver

Vitamin D
Eggs, liver, sardines, shiitake

Vitamin E
Fruits and vegetables, nuts and seeds, and seed oils"

Vitamin K
Leafy green vegetables, including spinach, egg yolks

THE NOVELS OF ANNE TYLER

If Morning Ever Comes (1964)
The Tin Can Tree (1965)
A Slipping-Down Life (1970)
The Clock Winder (1972)
Celestial Navigation (1974)
Searching for Caleb (1975)
Earthly Possessions (1977)
Morgan's Passing (1980)
Dinner at the Homesick Restaurant (1982)
The Accidental Tourist (1985)
Breathing Lessons (1988)
Saint Maybe (1991)
Ladder of Years (1995)
A Patchwork Planet (1998)
Back When We Were Grownups (2001)
The Amateur Marriage (2004)
Digging to America (2006)
Noah's Compass (2010)
The Beginner's Goodbye (2012)
A Spool of Blue Thread (2015)
Vinegar Girl (2016)
Clock Dance (2018)
Redhead by the Side of the Road (2020)

TOOLS FOR EVERY PURPOSE

A **ball-peen** hammer is used in metalworking. The distinctive feature is that it has two heads, one flat and one rounded (as opposed to flat, curved or otherwise shaped)

A **manual impact driver** is used to deliver a sudden, powerful rotational force when hit from behind with a hammer. Used to loosen tough nuts, bolts and screws

A **miter saw** allows the user to cut at a variety of angles with a spinning blade

A **dogleg reamer** is used to smoothly enlarge a hole

Stork beak pliers are used to reach into a hole to grab a small part from inside it

A **tooth chisel** with multiple teeth used to chisel rock

A **triple tap** is used by electricians to cut threads in holes and to clear out debris from holes in metal

A **cape chisel** is used by mechanics to scrape hardened dirt, paint or rust out of a narrow crevice

A **stubby nail eater** is an extra tough drill used to drill into wood that has (for instance) nails embedded in it

A rabbet is a 90 degree notch in a piece of woodwork: a **duplex rabbet plane** is a dual purpose plane that can be used to smooth the rabbet

An **egg beater drill** is powered, like an old fashioned egg beater, by turning the handle

A **flat bastard file** is simple tool with a double row of abrasive teeth used to shape metal

A **spud wrench** is used by plumbers to remove the wide fitting known as a spud, or by metalworkers to align two holes

A **shingle froe** is an old-fashioned tool used to split shingles and other types of lumber

A **halligan bar** is used by rescue workers to break into (for instance) burning buildings: effectively a hyped-up crow bar

A **pneumatic planishing hammer** is an air powered hammer used by metalworkers to smooth and polish metal

A Japanese **ryoba saw** is handheld with two opposing blades, one for cutting with and one against the grain

An **inflatable shim** is used by DIYers to prop open a window or door: it looks like a miniature airbag or blood pressure tester

A **torpedo level** is a small-scale spirit level, shaped like a torpedo and used inside small spaces

A **darby** is a simple handheld wooden tool used to flatten concrete

A **gorilla gripper** is a kind of clamp used to lift wooden sheets

An **ice pet** is an archaic kitchen tool for shaving ice

Big gus is actually the world's largest chainsaw: Michigan-based, it is a 23-foot machine powered by V-8 engines

DISEASES

1. Anthrax
2. Botulism
3. Cat-scratch disease
4. Chickenpox
5. Cholera
6. Common cold
7. Diphtheria
8. Gonorrhea
9. Legionnaires' disease
10. Leprosy
11. Malaria
12. Measles
13. Mumps
14. Scabies
15. Tetanus (Lockjaw)

THE MOVIES OF STANLEY KUBRICK

Fear and Desire, 1953
Killer's Kiss, 1955
The Killing, 1956
Paths of Glory, 1957
Spartacus, 1960
Lolita, 1962
Dr. Strangelove, 1964
2001: A Space Odyssey, 1968
A Clockwork Orange, 1971
Barry Lyndon, 1975
The Shining, 1980
Full Metal Jacket, 1987
Eyes Wide Shut, 1999

Three documentary shorts
Day of the Fight, 1951
Flying Padre, 1951
The Seafarers, 1953

Original storyline
A.I. Artificial Intelligence, 2001

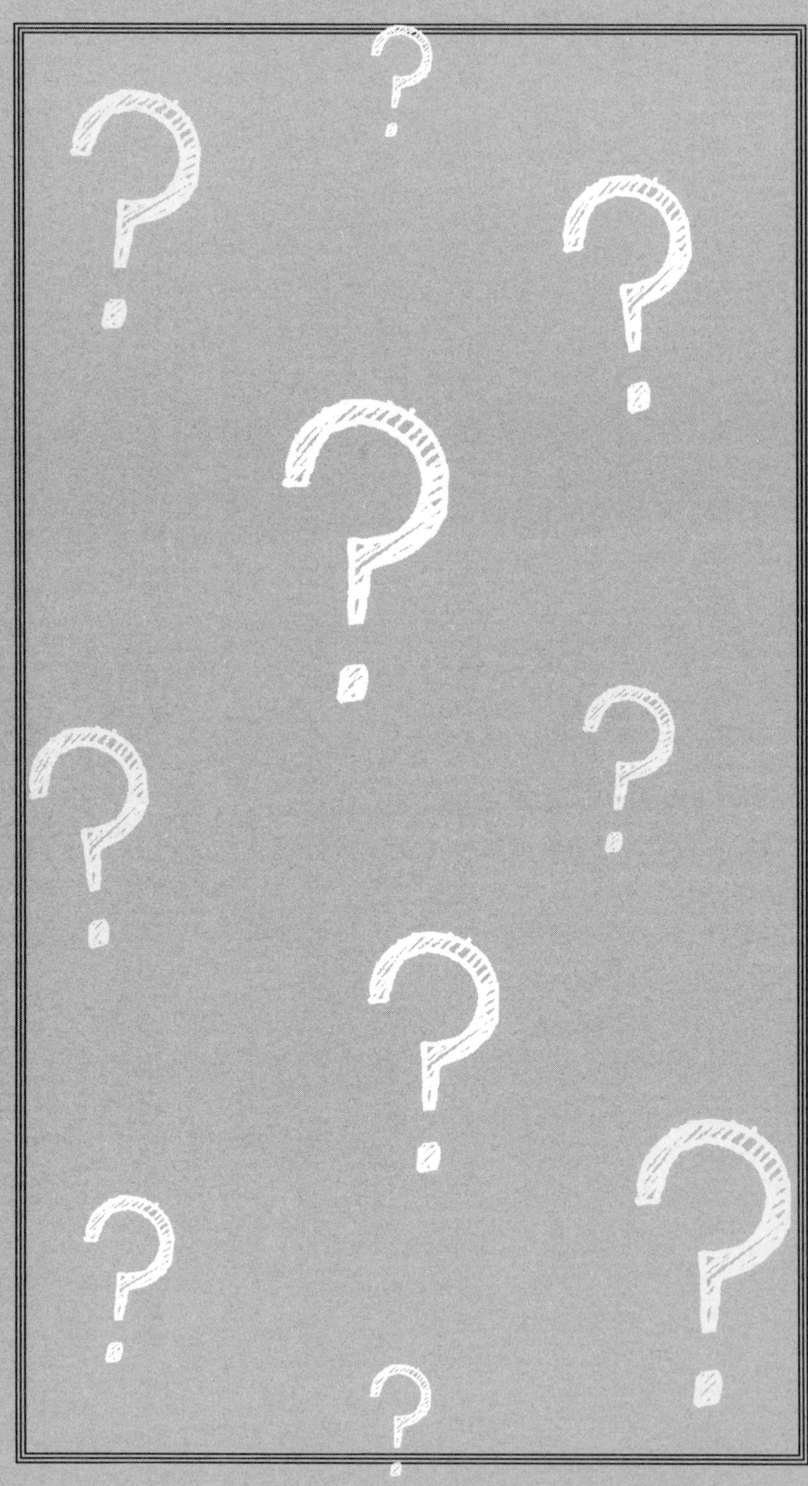

SO, HOW DID YOU DO?

WRITE YOUR NOTES HERE

WRITE YOUR NOTES HERE

WRITE YOUR NOTES HERE

WRITE YOUR NOTES HERE

WRITE YOUR NOTES HERE

WRITE YOUR NOTES HERE

WRITE YOUR NOTES HERE

WRITE YOUR NOTES HERE

WRITE YOUR NOTES HERE

WRITE YOUR NOTES HERE